MORE OF THE TILEHURST

WE REMEMBER

PUBLISHED BY

THE HISTORY OF TILEHURST GROUP

First Published in December 1999 by
The History of Tilehurst Group

Copyright The History of Tilehurst Group, 1999

No reproduction permitted without the prior
permission of the publisher:

The History of Tilehurst Group
19 Avington Close
Tilehurst, Reading RG31 5LW

ISBN   0 9531479 0 9

Front cover photograph: Turnham's Farm in 1974

Back cover photograph: Locally made air brick in wall of Turnham's Farm building 1974

(photographs by Peter Littledale)

Printed in Great Britain by
Parchment (Oxford)
Crescent Road
Cowley
Oxford OX4 2PB

CONTENTS

Introduction

Acknowledgements

Plan of School Road

Armour Road and Victoria Road
Mr Albert Illsley	1
Mrs Gwen Brereton	5
Miss Rose Burgess	9

Lyndhurst Road and Norcot Road
Mr Roy Stamp	11

Norcot Road and School Road
Mrs Doris Long	17
Mrs Olive Lascelles	23
Mrs Barbara Kirby	29
Mrs Lois Hedges	33
Mr George Critchell	37

Westwood Glen and Lower Armour Road
Mr Ken Englefield	39

Blundells Road
Mrs Joan Martin	43

St Michael's Road (formerly Church Road) and Wendover Way

Mrs Mavis Beakhouse 47

Mr Dennis Gill 51

Mr George Burgess 57

Mr Richard Beakhouse 61

Halls Road

Mrs Gladys Abery 71

Turnham's Farm

Mr Les Rixon 77

Chapel Hill

Mrs Dorothy Brocks 81

Mr Reginald Butler 83

Oak Tree Road

Mr Bill Stokes 89

Westwood Road

Mr Eric Borham 91

Mrs Doris Carter 93

Calcot

Mrs June Lush   95

Mr Les Hawkins   97

Memories of Park Lane School

by Mr George Critchell   99

Memories of Norcot School's Teachers   103

Photographs

Empire Day 1925 at Norcot School   27
(courtesy of Mrs D Long)

Class Photo : 4th form at Park Lane
School 1955   60
(courtesy of Mr R Beakhouse)

Turnham's Farm   79
(photo by Peter Littledale)

Park Lane School outing to Streatley Hill   101
circa 1935/6 *(courtesy of Mr D Gill)*

Teachers of Norcot School circa 1920   102
(courtesy of Mrs D Long)

INTRODUCTION

This second collection of memories evokes vivid images of life in Tilehurst during the first half of the twentieth century and beyond. In this book we have included extracts from twenty-four interviews and we would like to thank all those people who have been so willing to share their memories with us.

As in our previous book, it should be remembered that the information contained in these recollections is not necessarily factually correct, and should be accepted as the interviewees' perception of events, people and places.

We hope you enjoy reading More of the Tilehurst We Remember. For many it will bring back memories of a very different place from today's bustling, sprawling village and for those too young to recall those halcyon days it will paint a lively picture of life in Tilehurst and of those people who lived there from the very end of the Victorian age through to the post-war years.

ACKNOWLEDGEMENTS

We would like to thank the following people for their help and support with the production of this book:

- everyone who has given us interviews including those whose memories have not been used in this volume;

- Reading Local History Trust;

- Alan Hayden for his line drawings;

- Mrs Doris Long, Mr Richard Beakhouse and Mr Dennis Gill for allowing us to use their photographs;

- Mrs Ruth Terry for permission to use her map as a basis for the plan of School Road shown opposite page 1;

- Reading Borough Council and Newbury District Council (now West Berkshire District Council) for their support for our first book which has enabled us to produce this second volume;

- Duckworth and Kent Ltd, Armour Road, Tilehurst for their support; and

- all other people who have encouraged us and helped us in so many ways.

DIAGRAM OF AREA, AS
DESCRIBED BY MRS TERRY

	CHURCH ROAD	PARK LANE SCHOOL
		UNDERTAKER
		WESTWOOD ROAD
"LITTLE PLOUGH"	SCHOOL ROAD	A FIELD
		"THE PLOUGH"
		OLD NATIONAL SCHOOL
		SHOP
"THE LAURELS"		DR. HOSFORD
DENTIST		CHIMNEY-SWEEP
BLANCH		GENERAL SHOP, - MAY'S
RECREATION ROAD		METHODIST CHURCH
COX		
BOSWELL		DAIRY
"PACKER" ROBBINS		
CYCLES		PAPER SHOP
BISHOP		
WOND		ILLSLEY - CARRIER
'BRAGG', AT CORNER OF NORCOT ROAD		ARMOUR ROAD

MR ALBERT ILLSLEY
1905 - 1997

formerly of Armour Road

I was born in 1905. My father was killed on the Railway when I was only eight months old so my mother's people (Broadhurst) brought me up.

My Broadhurst grandparents lived in Polstead Road. The house is still there; it was no. 13 and now numbered 25. If you go down Polstead Road there are two archways - one is an open archway and lower down there is a blank one with bedrooms over the top. Only one side of the road was built on then.

My grandfather's name was George Ilsley and he lived in Armour Road about halfway between the corner and Wardle Avenue. My Uncle Harry had a shop opposite to where I live, Charlie Ilsley lives there now. Alf Ilsley, the carrier, now his place was in Norcot Road right opposite where the pet shop is now. There were just one or two biggish houses before the Borough Council houses were built there. He had stables and quite a bit of land at the back. There used to be a public footpath by the side of his ground that went down to the old pumping station in Gypsy Lane where the water was pumped up to Tilehurst. It was situated at the end of the brick kiln. There is still an old house there and the footings can be seen where the machinery stood. Another uncle lived in Recreation Road.

I went to Norcot School when I was five. It was up until you were fourteen but in the last four years we only did half day as we shared with Grovelands School. We used to go in the mornings, 9 'til 1 in the summer and afternoons, 1.30 to 5.30 in the winter so that the Grovelands children could get home in the light.

Tilehurst had two Post Offices; the original one was in School Road where the carpet shop used to be (the Postmaster was John Drew) where my job on Saturday mornings was to sit in the back and wait for telegrams to take round on my bike. Then we moved to Norcot Road and another one opened at the Triangle. Miss Townsend, a relation of Arthur Newbery, was the Postmistress.

I left school in 1919 and went to work at the brick kiln but got the sack for playing football one Saturday morning; they made bricks, but mostly tiles, roof tiles and pots, all handmade, fancy finials as well. Higgs and Colliers down Water Road mostly made bricks. Colliers were a bigger firm. They dug the clay at the back of where the Doctors' surgery and the Tyler's Rest is now in Norcot Road. My uncle Broadhurst worked at Colliers all his life.

I went to work for Huntley & Palmers; they said I could stay until Christmas, this was in July, and I stayed for 51 years! Had to walk to the Pond House to catch the tram - 2d return. No buses in Tilehurst. Braggs of Armour Road (where Hunsdon's Ice-Cream business is now situated) had the first couple of coaches; they were open-topped charabancs.

I was married in 1926. My wife came from Purley and we lived with my Broadhurst grandparents in Polstead Road. We came to Armour Road in June 1939. We rented it and bought it in 1951. The houses opposite called Surrey Villas and Polstead Road were built by Higgins from Caversham. My house was not new when we moved in, it used to be a dairy with stables at the bottom of the garden and a sign on the side wall which said, 'To the Dairy'.

I have been Treasurer and Secretary of the Poor Lands since 1947. When they had the Investiture of Tilehurst in 1905/6 nine hundred people lived up here. Theale and St George's were both originally in Tilehurst parish.

The land between Polstead Road and the Bird in Hand in Armour Road is Poor Land - where the allotments are now. Just this side of the public house was the baker Armstrong and he rented the land as far down as the Recreation Ground. He used to graze his horses there and before the 1914/18 War Tilehurst used to play football there.

When I was young we went down the bottom of Polstead Road and stood on the wall by the stream to watch the football. They didn't play football at the Recreation Ground until 1919 and then they took the land over for allotments. The Recreation Ground was farmland before 1897. Woodeson was there before then; it was open grazing land. In 1896/7 the Overseers of Tilehurst Parish asked the Trustees of Tilehurst Poor Lands if Woodeson would give up his lease so they could make it into a Recreation Ground to celebrate 60 years reign of Queen Victoria. Woodeson was paid £4 to end his lease. It is still rented to the Borough Council.

I remember Ford's Farm came up to Churchend Lane, where the Mormon Church is now and Norcot Farm (Minchin's) was on both sides of the Norcot Lane. Park Farm House which was where Mayfair is now has just been demolished. I knew it best when one of the Newbery family lived there. Part of the land was Poor Land at one time. Goodwin's Farm was down by St Michael's Church. Every Saturday morning before the first war I used to go down with our own can and buy skimmed milk from there at 2d a gallon. The farm had little tiny windows.

The Village Hall was opened on 10 January 1893. Two of Huntley & Palmers paid for the hall - Walter Palmer and GW Palmer. There was a public subscription. Liebenrood gave the ground and made the condition that no intoxicating drink was to be sold there. It was opened as a Reading Room; Benyon and a lot of people gave money.

Before National Health came in 1945, all Reading was divided into wards and each had their own Hospital collectors and we used to go round to as many as we could and they paid 2d per week for a man and wife and 3d for a family. We had our own Hospital Fete, banners and what not, once a year and I was brought up to take over the Tilehurst ward. There used to be quite a contest to see who could collect the most and I reckon my wife had the worst streets, Kentwood Hill and New Terrace. Willie Ball of Crescent Road was Treasurer and John Drew the Postmaster was the Chairman. After the 1939/45 war National Health came along and it was dropped. Nurse Bowles lived on the corner of Kentwood Terrace. She was the only nurse we had in Tilehurst and attached to Dr Carmody - Lynn Jones took over the practice. There was also Dr McCormer and Dr Fosbury in Westwood/Victoria Road.

Menpes had a nursery in Long Lane opposite Denefield School. They only grew tomatoes and cucumbers. They had six or eight cottages fairly old, beyond White Close and they were for the work people. Up in Tilehurst there was a nursery next door to me - Duffins.

Interviewed in February 1993

Catching the tram from the Pond House

MRS GWEN BRERETON
1919 - 1999

formerly of Armour Road

I was born in Armour Road. The Salvation Army was there. When it first started they had the village hall every other Sunday morning. Then Charlie Taylor the builder who lived in Armour Road built the Salvation Army hut just below us in Armour Road and after that it was a proper Corps. We were brought up there and my boy was dedicated there. My husband's family weren't Salvation Army and they weren't very happy about that so we had to have him christened in St Michael's. There was a chapel next door to it. But it was closed down and turned into a residential house. When I used to go in there they had this old chapel divided into rooms with curtains.

On Empire Day when I was at school we worked in the morning. Then we had the afternoon off and went down the Well Meadow which was on the left hand side of Pierce's Hill going down the hill. There was a well there. On the right hand side was the Barnet's paddock. We used to go down there in the afternoon. It was full of horse daisies and wild orchids. We'd spend all the afternoon in there. We always made for that on Empire Day. 24th May.

In Tilehurst everybody knew everybody else. Even up in the City you knew most of the people. At school the children from the City used to bring sandwiches and eat them in the bicycle shelters. We had to go home for lunch and I used to think how lovely it must be to bring sandwiches to school! Because they couldn't get back to school in time.

We had some lovely childhood days. I have some lovely memories of my childhood.

Collier's Hall was where they used to have the Band of Hope and different clubs. The wine shop in Norcot Road used to be Collier's clothing store. I remember buying a hoop from there! Behind there was a hall which must have belonged to them. It was called Collier's Hall. We used to go there for Band of Hope and the boys would have fretwork classes and my brother went there. Because there was nothing else up in this village. Hardly anyone had a wireless for years. I belonged to the White Ribboners first. My friend, they wouldn't have her because her father drank! You had to be teetotal to be a White Ribboner. When you got a certain age you trained to go to Band of Hope. Then Collier's Hall burned down.

I can remember when Amy Johnson came to visit some people in Long Lane. Where Fairford Road and all those houses are now, that was all fields then. This plane came down; we'd only just come home from school. Of course it was only a small plane, but to us it was huge. We saw it coming down lower and lower, but when we got there it had parked in this field and we could see it, but a policeman wouldn't let us get near it. I think it was Amy Johnson. That was so exciting. Give me those days back again!

We were never indoors when we were children. Mind you it was safer then. I feel sorry for the children today. They cannot roam like we did. We went off for hours and hours and didn't come back until it was dark. We used to take sandwiches and home-made lemonade and we made our own fun. It was a lovely life although most people had very little money.

Philips the blacksmith was almost on the corner of Armour and Lower Armour Roads. My dad used to take his horse there to be shoed. The original Bird in Hand was lower down before they built the present one and the Butcher's Arms was a tiny old-fashioned place run by a brother and two or three sisters. Their name was Hunt. I used to go there with my friend to get her dad's beer in a jug and you had to go round the side. I remember the men used to sit on seats in a little porch thing outside in the summer and they'd let her have the beer because they knew her father. But he still went down there at night drinking; this was only his Sunday lunchtime one!

I remember Mrs Barnet from Westwood House; if anyone was sick or poorly she would give them a note to take to the butchers for meat and she would allow two pints of milk a week say for a month and all other things. I remember my sister when my dad was dying taking this big jug down and they'd fill it with soup. Oh she was marvellous, Mrs Barnet was. They had a blind daughter, Mary, and she'd go round in a dog cart. They liked to think that they were the squires of the village. We always thought that the square mile was from the Triangle down to Armour Hill round Armour Hill, back up Kentwood Hill and round back to the Triangle. And they used to call that the square mile, I don't know why. But that was her province. Anybody in that area she was marvellous to them. My mother always praised her. I wasn't quite nineteen when Mervyn, my eldest one, was born and my mother took the baby over to show Mrs Bridges in the village shop and Mrs Barnet was in there with her ear trumpet. You know, she came over to see me. "You're now't but a child yourself!" she said. Now she allowed us two pints of milk and a dozen eggs a week for a month. Now I didn't really need it because my husband was working. But that's how she was. She spoke very much like a man, very abrupt, but when it came to doing things for those people in the village she was wonderful. In the autumn she let us go in the paddock and climb the trees to get the conkers down and she'd send out bags of apples for us to eat.

We always called the house 'Lady Eldon's' because she had lived there before the Barnets.

Interviewed in May 1998

Everyone kept pigs and chickens and grew their own vegetables

MISS ROSE BURGESS
1895 - 1998

formerly of Victoria Road

My father built this house and I moved in here when I was a year old. I remember we had no sewerage or running water. There was a well in the back garden which is still there and a pump over the kitchen sink. We had two oil lamps and used candles. Gas arrived later. Victoria Road was very puddly and frequently under water. There were very few houses in Victoria Road, I can remember nos 17 and 19 which my father built, the Nursery House on the corner and the Post Office on the corner of Victoria Road and Armour Road. Everyone had long gardens and kept pigs and chickens and also grew their own vegetables. My mother kept a sow. We didn't do much shopping as we were reasonably self-sufficient. I remember during the war taking fruit to the Village Hall where there was a canning machine*.

I started school at 3 years of age. The bell at Park Lane School used to ring and when it stopped you were late! My mother used to comb my hair at the back door, searching for fleas and the bell was ringing and ringing and I dreaded it would stop before I could get to school. Lots of children had fleas and I can remember sitting behind one girl and watching the fleas moving about on her hair and hoping I wouldn't catch any as my mother would be cross.

I used to run errands for the lady next door. I would race along as I knew what my reward would be - a slice of Huntley & Palmers fruit cake - delicious!

I left school when I was 14 years old and was apprenticed to the Millinery Department at Heelas. I didn't pay anything for the apprenticeship but I didn't get any wages either. On my first day I was told to buy some pincers; these were needed as hats were made on frames in those days. I remember there was a long table, and the older women didn't make life easy for us young school leavers. We worked a very long day and if something special was happening we had to work even longer hours.

interviewed in June 1993

* *The canning machine referred to was apparently owned by the Tilehurst Women's Institute. The period of time it was in use is uncertain, but definitely during the 1939/45 war. It was kept in Mr Albert Illsley's attic and brought round to the Village Hall in Victoria Road when the fruit from the local people's gardens was ripe. The ladies brought their fruit round, were handed tins which they packed themselves and labelled, all information being written down so that there could be no mistakes made. During the day certain members put the lids on and the whole lot was sterilised. In the evening the ladies returned to collect their goods.*

Information kindly supplied by Mrs Joyce Parkin

MR ROY STAMP
born 1931

formerly of Lyndhurst Road and Norcot Road

I was born and brought up in Lyndhurst Road in Lower Tilehurst. To get to Norcot School from Lyndhurst Road we'd go up Romany Lane and come out by the Tyler's Rest pub and walk up the hill. If there was no gypsies in the field then we could go up into Thirlmere Avenue from St Mary Magdelene's Church. The church used to be down behind the shops in the Oxford Road. It was quite a walk, especially in winter

When I was young you weren't allowed up into McIlroy's Park if the gypsies was in the bottom field.

My aunties and uncles worked at Higgs Potteries in Water Road. As you went up Grovelands Road and into Water Road right on the bend on the right all the chimney sweeps used to go and empty their soot there and anybody could come and take the soot to put on their gardens. I remember having to walk all the way there from Lyndhurst Road to get a bag of soot for Dad to put on his garden! And it was a fair old way. And they were beautiful allotments and in them days kids didn't dare steal anything from them 'cos you'd get a beating from your parents. They were very strict. There was a code - you never touched a man's allotment. We had allotments then just above St Mary Magdelene's Church, that was at the end of Lyndhurst where they've got the little community centre now. In those days you'd go down there and there was the Church, the hall and the shops at the bottom of Weald Rise just opposite Waitrose. We used to go to that Church and if you went there and looked fit you had to pump the organ! They used to grab you as you went in!

From where the Tyler's Rest is now down to the bottom of Norcot Hill on the left that used to be Minchin's Farm. Sometimes you could cut a corner off by going across the farm but one of the farm workers used to get on his grey horse and chase you! It was a damn great horse and he used to chase us all over the field! Where Broomfield Road is now that was all farmland. At the bottom of Romany Lane where it goes into Norcot Road there used to be another piece of waste ground and a chap in there with a horse and cart. He was called London and was the vegetable man and used to go round the estates. He'd sell everything.

I remember Scrivener building the houses in Thirlmere Avenue when I was a child, must have been in the late thirties. There was a chap who lived in Lyndhurst Road and he was a night watchman up there and he only had one arm. He used to do the patrols up there.

Saturday or Sunday night we used to go up to the Bird in Hand and the Butcher's Arms in Tilehurst. My parents would go in the Bird in Hand and there was a big cherry tree in the garden and we would climb that. We would just sit there and if they came out with a packet of crisps we was lucky! Just below there on the left, facing the entrance to Arthur Newbery Park was a little shop called Dawsons. He was another one who was always in the Bird in Hand.

Opposite us, the man who done the blinds in Reading, the shop awnings, he was called Donald Gray and he was the blind maker for Reading. It didn't matter where you went in Reading if you had a blind or awning up, it was made by Donald Gray. He lived in Lyndhurst Road.

During the war every house was asked to take in evacuees from London. We had a couple stay with us with one child. In the house we had a kitchen, a room we used to call the back room and the lounge and they had that room only. They lived, ate, slept in there but obviously had the use of the toilet and all the other facilities. But their cooking was all different 'cos I think they were Jewish people. But we had to have them during the war. Down by the Bell (it's called The Restoration now) underneath the pub, there used to be the air raid wardens' centre for all that area. All the gas masks used to be kept there. There was a big ARP post up at the water tower near Norcot School and they had spotters up at the big water tower near the Bear Inn.

Ranikhet Camp used to go from the back of the allotments up into Tilehurst and we used to go up to the newsagents, just before you get to the White House on the left there, and buy half a dozen evening newspapers and then go round Ranikhet Camp saying we were paper boys. So we sold the papers for more than their cost - the Americans would always pay more and we got into the camp free of charge. One of the chaps was in the 101st Airborne Division and somewhere I have got a letter saying,

> 'To Whom It May Concern,
> I have given this German rifle to Roy Stamp for safe keeping.'

And it had his name and address on it. I've got that somewhere. I took the rifle home and we had it hanging in the hallway. Mother got a bit worried with all the ammunition what with Dad working nights so we went down to Scours Lane where the lido used to be and threw all the ammunition in the river. In the end we handed the rifle into the police station.

In McIlroy's Park there used to be a big underground shelter and the little hut for the watchman. During the war some houses had the Anderson air raid shelters but in Lyndhurst Road we had the ones built in the street. Each house was allocated a shelter. After a while they reinforced them. When we were kids we'd go inside and show films for 1d each! In them days you didn't go far, your parents could always look out in the street and see you. But on Sundays you didn't go out in the street unless you had your Sunday clothes on.

The ice storage place in Scours Lane near the Bell used to be done out in camouflage and I think that got machine-gunned during the war. There was hardly any work going on in the cold storage place during the war, we think they used it for stock-piling, dried eggs and the like.

We had street parties after the war and everybody enjoyed themselves and it was a wonderful atmosphere. And everybody helped to clean up afterwards.

I used to deliver papers for the shop at the bottom of Kentwood Hill. My paper round was every house in Kentwood Hill - up one side and down the other. I used to go up to the farm, deliver the papers to the farm and she always had a box outside with fruit in it for anyone to help themselves and I used to put whatever I wanted in my paper bag to take home. I got 5s a week for that, 7 days a week. When I first started work I got 18s 4d. and that was up at Everetts up in Wantage Road just next to the Spread Eagle. They used to make aircraft parts, sheet metal work. My mother had 14s of my money!

We moved to the caravan site in Church End Lane about 43 years ago. Coopers owned the caravan site and his relation also owned the little farm up by St Michael's Church there. I think before then it used to be an orchard because all our gardens had beautiful apple trees and plum trees. We never went without fruit. There used to be big hoardings along there. At the back of the caravan site you could get onto the bridle path which went higher up Church End Lane. That was the best time of our married life, when we lived there. The atmosphere was just wonderful.

No-one ever locked their doors in those days. In fact you couldn't open Beryl's mum's front door with a key anyway because the amount of Brasso she put on it got all gunged up and they had to change the lock! When we was courting, she used to go to bed and she had an electric stove and she always put the kettle half on and half off so that when I brought Beryl home she could make me a cup of tea and I wouldn't have to hang around too long. She lived in Whitley down by Gillettes and I was in the caravan and she used to give me a lemonade bottle filled with hot water so that when I got home I could have a shave and a wash.

The woman who owned the site, Mrs Cooper, had a little shop there and a club where we used to go and enjoy ourselves in the evenings, table tennis, darts and things like that.

When you wanted a bath on the caravan site you had to go in and stoke the boiler up in the wash house. You'd use old shoes or anything you could lay your hands on to burn. You'd heat the water, put your bath in there, fill it up and put curtains up at the window and have your bath!

Cooper who owned the caravan site had three sons and his sons done all the haulage for Tilehurst Potteries. They'd go into the potteries, load up with tiles, take their lorries back to Church End Lane, park them and next morning off they'd go. One of them got killed down the Oxford Road one morning as he was driving his lorry down there. He had a smash and got killed.

When we lived on the caravan site the butcher used to come to us every day from the Oxford Road by the Bell. We'd order our meat each day for the next day.

There was Rosier's the florist in Blundells Road and when we were in the caravan a little old lady had that and she used to make her own cheese. It was beautiful, you cut it and it just crumbled. We used to buy loads of cheese from her.

We had no running water in the caravan; we had to go out for the toilet and the wash house. I was in bed one morning and the wife came running in and said, 'Quick! Taff's caravan's on fire!' I got out of bed, it was raining hard and his caravan was on fire. In fifteen minutes it burned to the ground. All that was left was the shell and I've never seen anything go up like it. When they came up to take the debris away, the council wanted to charge him one shilling per dustbin for the rubbish they took away. But this man had lost everything.

After the caravan site we moved to Southcote. We've never lived anywhere else. My next-door-neighbour Arthur Roberts had an uncle Steve Jackson who worked at Higgs and remembers cleaning the chimneys on a Sunday by firing a double-barrelled shotgun up them.

Interviewed in August 1998

Walking the pig and goat!

MRS DORIS LONG MBE
(formerly GASH, nee BAREFOOT)
born 1915

formerly of School Road and Norcot Road

I am Doris Long, formerly Doris Barefoot, now aged eighty four. My father owned the cycle shop in School Road.
He originally came from Oxford. He and Billy Morris started off just the same, bicycles and so on in Oxford, but Mr Morris was a hard-headed businessman and went on to own Morris Motors and became a millionaire. He became Lord Nuffield and gave money to the Royal Berkshire Hospital and all the new Nuffield buildings were named after him. But my father was easy-going and would allow people to owe him money.
Through a relative, my father heard that a cycle shop was badly needed in Tilehurst so we moved there when I was about two years old.
We sold wirelesses and jewellery as well as bicycles. My father could do anything really. Anything that didn't work people brought to him to fix. If someone brought a bike in to have a puncture mended which cost sixpence in those days, he'd go all round the bike and mend their brakes and anything else and still only charge them sixpence. And he often used to mend people's bikes and leave them outside the shop until they came to fetch them. They'd come and fetch them and never come in and pay him.

I used to be the envy of all the children in Tilehurst 'cos my dad used to make lots of toys. He made me something that was like a scooter but with a piece coming up and a saddle. My mother used to grumble because I wore one shoe out on a scooter you see, so he put this saddle on so I could go with two feet and I wore both shoes out!

He used to make me all sorts of things; he was very clever with his hands. I used to have two little birds at one time, a goldfinch and a linnet. They were very tame and he made lots of little toys for them, a roundabout, a see-saw etc and they used to love it. I used to take them round to the old people's houses to show them, making sure they had no cats about and that all the windows and doors were shut! These little birds loved it and they seemed to know which thing they had to go on next. It was amazing really. Tim and Jenny I used to call them. I had a collecting box for the PDSA. I've collected for the PDSA since about 1930 I think.

Next door to our shop in School Road lived a blind man, Mr Brown, who made wicker baskets and doormats to sell. He was subsidised by St Dunstans *(charity that supports those blinded in the service of their country)*. I used to sit and read to him whilst he was working when I was a girl. Next door to him was a greengrocer, Mr Robins, who delivered his fruit and veg in a cart pulled by a little mule, and next to him was a butcher, Mr Boswell, who used to slaughter the animals at the back of his shop. I hated Mondays when I could hear the pigs screaming.

When I was about eight or nine I had a baby goat given me by Mr Goble, the local lamplighter and chimney sweep. I called her Nancy and reared her on the bottle. When she was older I used to take her every morning before school around Victoria Park, where she would nibble the shoots on the hedge which I believe is still there.

I attended Norcot Road School when Mr Saxby was headmaster and Mr Saul taught the older children. He was very keen on sport and trained us for athletics. I became girl School Champion in 1926 and Jack Deverall was the boys' champion. He later played for Reading Football Club.

Before I became good at athletics I was really scared of Mr Saul as were many others. He used to throw pieces of chalk at us with deadly accuracy if we weren't attending. He used to call me

"Pussyfoot"! Opposite the school was a little sweet shop run by Miss Munday where we used to spend our pocket money.

I was friendly with the Beasley family who had the bakery in Recreation Road and each Good Friday I would go to help with the hot cross buns. These were delivered early in the morning still piping hot to people living around

During the war my father was not allowed to enlist as everyone needed him. There was Dr Carmody who lived in School Road, who later had a pony and trap, and Nurse Godden, who lived on top of Kentwood Hill. She relied on a bicycle to visit all the patients. Also those people who could afford it used cycles to get to and from work as there were no buses that ran to Tilehurst. We had to walk to the Pond House to get a tram into Reading. My father died in 1946, but my mother lived until she was ninety-nine.

On the corner of Recreation Road and School Road lived Charlie White, a tailor. He owned a little terrier dog called Major and next to him and adjoining Lainsbury's Nurseries lived a family named Matthews. They owned a little dog called Jack who used to come and call for me to take him for a walk. He would sit patiently waiting outside the door. Opposite was a newsagents run by Mr Sparkes who rode a three-wheeled tricycle. Then Mr Illsley moved with the carrier's cart from Norcot Road and later he had the first petrol pumps in Tilehurst. Next door to him lived PC Groves who had five children. Further on next door to the Wesleyan Chapel was a dairy owned by Billy Manning. He delivered milk in a horse and cart and some evenings and weekends I was allowed to borrow Dolly the horse and go riding. That was my first job, doing the book-keeping there. Later I worked in Shire Hall in the children's department, my boss being Mr Cripps who lived in Church Road.

I well remember Mr Stacey the dentist who took out my first tooth without an anaesthetic as I had an abscess under it. His two daughters, Sybil and Muriel belonged to the Girl Guides where I was also a member. We all went to camp at Lyme Regis once in Mr Illsley's carrier van. They were very friendly with Trixie Chadwick who lived opposite and taught the piano.

There was a family of Butlers in the City and one of the sons, Mark, played for Tilehurst Football Team. I also remember a girl who lived down there who was well known for having fleas in her hair! I used to sit behind her in school and you could see them walking about! When Nitty Nora came round she'd be away for a few days!

I was a Sunday School teacher at the Methodist Church for several years. I started off as a pupil and then went on to teach. I remember I had boys and I would bribe them with those little text cards. I 'd go down the market and there was a Mr Matthews who had a stall where he sold these text cards and I would buy them and if the boys were good they got a text card, but if they weren't they didn't get one!

I lost my first husband in the war and my father died shortly after so my mother was left on her own. I was living at Newbury at that time and travelling to my work at Shire Hall, Reading every day, so it was the sensible thing to move back with my mother in Tilehurst, so I did. Then we sold up the shop and moved down Norcot Road.

My interest in animal welfare really started when I went with a friend to the police station because she had lost her dog and in those days they only kept the animals for a week and then they destroyed them. She said, "Come with me, Dot, to the police station to see if my dog is there!" It wasn't, but there was a little brown dog with such pathetic eyes and I said to the policeman that I was sure it would be claimed soon. He told me that it was going to be put down in the morning. I went back to the office and kept thinking about that dog all the time. As I was working all day at that time I didn't really want a dog, but I couldn't stand the thought of that little dog being put down. So I rang the police and said, "Don't put down the little brown dog and I'll come and collect it tomorrow." So I went and collected it in the morning before I went to the office. I thought I'd keep it for a bit until I found it a new home to save it being put down. And that dog, when I was in the office with it, followed me everywhere and it sat and looked up at me and the girls all said, "You're not going to part with that dog, Dot, you'll never part with that dog." I replied, "Oh yes I shall. I can't keep a dog." My mother wasn't very keen on dogs at that time. But anyway I did keep it; I couldn't part with it. Then that got me thinking that if only somebody would take an animal in and look after it for a little while and find it a new home it would save so many of them being put down and that's what I started doing - ringing the police and asking if they had one that was going to be put down.

Then I adopted a one-eyed pony. He'd been terribly ill-treated. Ever-so nervous he was. At that time I had Cherry, my adopted little girl, and she kept wanting a pony. So we had this one on loan from a Home. By that time I'd moved down to Norcot Road and we had this great big piece of land at the back of the old hoardings. I thought it was a shame as I had a big stable and all this land so I decided to get something to keep him company. So then we got a goat and the animal sanctuary built from there. Then the police and the RSPCA got to know me. I remember one day we could hear some pigs squealing and we went out to the door and there were two policemen coming in and one had got a baby pig under one arm and the other had a baby goat. They had been found wandering somewhere and they never were claimed. I had to rear them on the bottle, they were little tiny things. We called them Pinky and Perky. I made little harnesses for them and Cherry used to take them for walks on leads. Dear little things they were.

We used to visit Daneshill every spring. It belonged to Arthur Newbery and then Smith of Smith's Coaches bought it and we'd go up there on a Sunday when it was open, walk round all the grounds and all these rhododendrons, they were beautiful.

Sometimes we'd go on trips up the river on Maynard's Steamers. I've got a photo of me on one of their steamers.

Smith's coaches used to go to Hayling Island three times a week for day-trippers. They came on Saturdays, Sundays and Wednesdays. We used to have to pay a penny to come across the old wooden bridge onto the island.

I ran the animal sanctuary in Tilehurst for twenty years and re-homed over 18,000 animals.

Interviewed in March 1999

Who's keeping an eye on whom?

MRS OLIVE LASCELLES
(nee GROVES)
born 1909

formerly of School Road

I was born in Reading; my father was in the Reading Police Force and when I was about five years old he was transferred to School Road, Tilehurst.

My father policed Tilehurst for many years until his retirement. My older brother also joined the Police Force and became an inspector.

I attended Norcot School and one of my memories is of Empire Day when I had to wear red, white and blue. My outfit was all made from crepe paper and I carried a flag. I stood next to "Britannia". I then went on to Wilson Central School, having passed my 11+ and in those days the classes were segregated. The only time I had the cane was at Norcot School because I couldn't remember the music alphabet!

At first the family went to St Michael's Church, but it was a long way and as each baby came we didn't want to go that far, and we had the Methodist Church opposite. The Minister at St Michael's was Cooper-Smith, and he had two maiden sisters who brought round almanacs, and they used to storm about us going over there.

When Ralph (my husband) lived in Armour Road his mother and father were important people at the Methodist Church. His father was organist and his mother was choir leader. Ralph was later organist at Caversham Heights for about 35 years. My friend Maisie Matthews and I were in the choir and we used to have choir practice in Mrs Lascelles' lounge. One day we did an awful thing there! There was this fish and chip van that came round and we only collected some chips on our way to choir practice (and Mrs Lascelles was very much the Duchess) and Maisie kept nudging me to take a chip from her pocket. Mother went to Maisie and told her it wasn't the done thing, chips in Mrs Lascelles' lounge!

Mrs Kenchington who lived next door got up all the concerts for the Church.

When my father was a policeman he cycled round Tilehurst all day keeping his eyes and ears open. In those days we children were frightened of schoolmasters and frightened of the police. We had the Zeppelin in the First War come over for one thing - and my father had to go out immediately. They were plucking a chicken - we kept chickens in the back garden. We had chicken so often, it was our mainstay.

We had that awful 'flu epidemic in the First World War, I was probably nine or ten years old and the only one in that big family left on my feet. I had to go and get the wood and light the fires and the awful thing was that so many people died and you kept seeing the funerals passing. It was a dreadful time really. Mrs Skinner, another policeman's wife had several children but she brought things round for me to feed the family.

When we were at 14 School Road we kept chickens and my father shared a pig with somebody. As the butcher was opposite he used to do the necessary. My father was a good gardener and grew his own vegetables. You wonder when they had the time to do everything, mother making clothes for all of us. Many years later we had an outing and went over the new Police Station, and there was my father's initials for his wages - £2 per week - honestly how did they manage? Of course they had a house and the uniform, but not much else.

We used to go across the Moor to Smewings Farm and get skimmed milk as children, and you know it was an awfully long walk.

I was an apprentice at Heelas - as cashier in the Accounts Department. I sat in that box up high and pulled the string. I had a three year apprenticeship and was paid half a crown the first year and five shillings the second. I answered an advertisement for Huntley & Palmers and they offered me £2 per week! I said to my mother, "I can't be worth £2 per week!" It was fun there - it was a mixed office - but some of the men remembered when it was only men. I used to cycle to work, but on one occasion I got caught in the tram lines and had to let the tyres down to get free.

My husband Ralph was born in Tilehurst I believe. His mother owned two houses, "Grafton" and "Deersville" down the end of Recreation Road. His grandparents lived in one, but when the grandfather died my husband's mother who lived in Armour Road next to Lynn Jones, looked after the grandmother.

Ralph started on the railway - his father had a good job on the railway you see and it was the thing to do. Then he went to work for Quartermain's before he was called up and when he came back he decided he was definitely going to start his own business. Mr Herbert lived on the corner of Armour and Lower Armour Road and Ralph went along to the house to ask if he had a radio magazine where they advertised for people. Mrs Herbert said Ralph was the answer to their prayers as Mr Herbert had died and she had no-one to run the business. So that is how Herbert and Lascelles, the electrical business, started. The shop was in St Mary's Butts, before the shopping centre was built. My husband fought successfully not to have it pulled down as it was so old.

Margaret Spencer ran the poultry farm at Kentwood; her sister Peggy was a nurse and Muriel Spencer started the Highlands School in October 1929. Muriel died very suddenly on March 1st 1939, she was only in her early thirties. She had made such a good thing of the Highlands School it seemed so tragic.

Margery Haddock was at school with me and lived next door to us in Westwood Road. She was the daughter of Haddocks the builder, who built so much of the property in Tilehurst - you would always see in the advertisements, 'Haddock built' which was always an incentive knowing it was *well built*.

As regards the shops in Tilehurst, starting at the water tower in Norcot Road, there was Oxford's Haberdashery and Ladies' Outfitters - I know we went there for our hats about 2/11d. Poor Mrs Oxford always had chilblains, it was a cold old shop. He called on us because we owed him a farthing! I know I was sent down there for some needles. My mother was a terrific needlewoman, well she had to make all our clothes. I got all the way back and they were rusty and she made me go back again with them. Then there was Vivian's the butchers; Roy Collier, they kept the Gents' Outfitters. He was a school teacher and his sister was Kathleen Manning. Kathleen said, "Gosh, you were our salvation with all your children!" Then there was Milwards shoe shop, next door the Post Office (Drews), Warner's the barber, then Bragg the Grocer. We only had half day school in the First War and my brother went as an errand boy at Braggs. On the corner was Marshall the greengrocers, Wands the sweet and tobacco shop, then Bishops the chemist. Barefoot's was next, the cycle repair shop. My first bike cost 7/6d. it was one of those thick framed ones. Cox the sweet shop, Lainsbury the nurseries. I was at school with the Lainsburys and the Laileys, they were all related. Then there was the police house where we lived, Stacey the dentist (Muriel and Sybil played tennis with us). The Laurels, now the library and clinic, and the Post Office by the monument.

On the opposite side of the road to the Laurels in School Road there was Misses Roberts' private school where Ralph and his sister attended. We always thought of them as arsenic and old lace because they always wore lavender colours. They told their pupils not to play with the village children, all snooty. Yet I used to see Jean Talford, she went there as well, and we always had our noses pressed against Mrs Cox's window to see what we could spend our farthings on! She used to say, "Daddy said I mustn't buy rubbish!" Then there was Miss Bowles the District Nurse, she was a skinny little thing with those high collars.

Many of the business people in Reading came to Tilehurst to live. There was Sarjents, the tool and steel cutlery firm in West St; Newberys at Daneshill, (the son had Park Farm); McIlroy who had the big departmental store; Dawson the bakers; Alf Smith and Lucy - he was a Rotarian and they used to put up a marquee and we had some lovely times there; Busby of Oaktree Road, a wood firm. McIlroy, Alf Smith and Busby were all Mayors of Reading. In Newbery Park the old Tilehurst Library building was originally the Little White Ribbon Hall, and then of course there used to be the village hall where we had dances, films and socials. I used to go to the dances but never had a boy partner, always danced with a girl. Francis the builders were in Westwood Road. We played tennis at the Lloyds' in Wardle Avenue.

Ralph was President of the Radio Trade and organised the annual TV and Radio Shows at Reading Town Hall. Richard Dimbleby, Raymond Glendenning, Eric Robinson, Mary Malcolm and Barry Edgar were celebrities at these shows.

Interviewed in September 1996

Empire Day 1925 at Norcot School. Nellie Skinner, the policeman's daughter is 'Brittania'

Palmer's Stores in School Road

MRS BARBARA KIRBY
(nee MORLEY)
born 1916

formerly of School Road

My name is Barbara Kirby, nee Morley. We came to Tilehurst from Wanborough (a village four miles from Swindon) in 1932. I was 16, my brother Sam was 13 and my sister Ann 1 year old.

Jobs were few and my father thought buying a shop would be work for us all, so he bought Palmer's Stores, 30 School Road, Tilehurst. The shop was run by Miss Palmer and her brother, who was blind (or almost). There was a mother also blind and confined to a chair and a father. Palmer's Stores was owned by a Mr May before the Palmers - I think they said he was a baker.

The kitchen/sitting room at the back of the building was just one floor and, I think, originally used as the bakehouse. In the place that we used as a dining room there was a fireplace and we were told that behind it was the original oven.

The shop when we took it over was very small, but my father had the room at the side taken into the shop so it was quite a decent size for that time. My father bought a refrigerator, not many about then. We put a notice outside when it was hot, swanking that things like cooked meat, bacon, butter, etc was kept fresh. Sides of bacon went in also.

Miss Palmer delivered groceries in a handcart which she pushed round the village. I was sent up to Tilehurst a week earlier than the family to learn about the shop. I stayed with Mr and Mrs Goodger, 53 Westwood Road, and their daughter Molly who was a teacher at Grovelands School. Mr Goodger was a verger at St Michael's Church. Soon after we took over the shop, Molly Goodger and I joined a tennis club. It was called Woodland Lawn Tennis Club near Woodland Drive. Bill Broom was a member. I told him we were having our shop enlarged and he said, "I could do that, I am a shop fitter." He lived in Beechwood Avenue.

I went with Miss Palmer delivering goods in the handcart. When the day before moving came, she told me to go round on my own. I was only 16 and I was embarrassed. I got as far as Recreation Road and two women pointed at me. I expect they just meant I was one of the new people moving in, but I thought they were laughing at me, so I ran to the telephone box and 'phoned a friend in Wanborough and he came up and we delivered the groceries in his car. My father bought a bicycle with a large basket in front for my brother to deliver the groceries. He gave the handcart to the Boy Scouts to take their camping things from place to place.

When we started in the shop times were very hard, very little money about and of course the people didn't get any help from the Government. Actually it seemed to get worse. People used to come in and get things on tick, then we had a job to get the money in. Everything was sold loose. Biscuits in large tins, eggs (people would come in for one egg, two eggs). We sometimes bought butter in a ½ cwt piece and mother would be out in the kitchen bashing it about and weighing it up. Apparently we had some scales that were faulty and along came the Weights & Measures people; somebody must have reported it. They were very understanding. But Mother got very worked up about it.

My brother Sam went to Norcot School for a year. My sister Ann went to school in 1936 in a house in Armour Road run by a lady called Mrs Gale. She also went to a dancing teacher in Kentwood Hill - Miss Stockley, 179 Kentwood Hill, Tylehurst School of Dancing. I can remember my sister doing tap dancing all over the place at home.

We made friends with the Staceys opposite at no. 51. Frederick Stacey was a dentist, also Mrs Stacey, Sybil (now Mrs Millard) was the younger daughter and Muriel the eldest. Muriel worked with her father at his surgery in Zinzan Street. Both the girls were excellent pianists. Sybil was a piano teacher and played with an orchestra in one of the restaurants in town. Muriel was more into modern music and sometimes played in a dance band. There were lots of dance bands then. They were needed for the many dance halls. Sybil Stacey later played in an orchestra in the restaurant above McIlroys in Reading, until war started in 1939. Trixie Chadwick in School Road was also a good pianist, like the Stacey girls. She played in the orchestra at the Palace Theatre in Reading.

Next door to the Staceys was a large house with grounds called the Laurels. It later became a school. The Groves lived next door to the Staceys on the other side. Mr Groves had been a policeman. There was quite a large family. On the corner of Recreation Road lived Charles White, a tailor, next to Lainsbury's Nursery. Mr Illsley the carrier was at no. 14 and his son Tom Illsley lived opposite at no. 15/17. We put bets on big races with him (although it was illegal to hand your money over for that in those days). He was an extremely nice man.

Doris Barefoot (the daughter of Mr Barefoot who had the cycle shop) was a friend of mine. She helped in our shop for while. She was very fond of animals. After the war she started an animal sanctuary in Norcot Road. She received an MBE for her good work. She was Doris Gash by then; later she married again, her name now is Mrs Long. Mr Barefoot's shop was taken over by a boot repairer.

Teenagers called a meeting in the old National School near the Plough in School Road to form a club and discussions took place about stopping young ones wandering about. Teenage boys and girls would wander down Broad Street and Friar Street, boys one way, girls the opposite way, and flirting on the way. It was thought that cinemas should open on Sundays to give them something to do. Cinemas were allowed to open soon afterwards. Dances were held in the Village Hall in Victoria Road, we had great times. No canned music in those days, always dance bands. We girls would hope to be escorted home by one of the boys. Another hall was down somewhere between Kentwood and Norcot. We would walk home after the dances across some fields near the Potteries.

At Park Farm there was a model steam engine on railway lines, large enough for kids to ride on. He would have fetes ending with fireworks. His father gave Arthur Newbery Park to the village.

The steam engine was made by William Lush who, I have been told by his grandson, lived in Armour Road and then 10 Norcot Road in the 1920's.

A mother and daughter came to live in Tilehurst from London and one day I took her for a walk in Sulham Woods and we went past a field with lots of cows and she said, "Oh, there's some bulls!." I had to explain the difference between bulls and cows! Then on the way back these bats all came swooping round and she was screaming her head off, and I said that they wouldn't hurt her. Later she told a friend that she liked me but that I was a bit of a country bumpkin!

In 1937 my father was diagnosed as a diabetic. Later he had trouble with his hip for which he was given the wrong treatment, which later we found had put his hip right out and he became crippled. With customers having difficulty paying us, we were having trouble making ends meet in the business, so we decided to sell the shop. An elderly man came up and said, "I hear you want to sell your business!" He moved in but didn't stay long and then Mr Petry took over.

Buses came as far as the Plough, School Road. Some time later they went to the Bear Inn. When the war came I noticed it didn't say 'Tilehurst' on the front, just 'Bear Inn'. Place names were kept secret.

Interviewed in March 1999

MRS LOIS HEDGES
(nee AYRES)
1903 - 1995

formerly of School Road

I came to Tilehurst when I was ten years old. My dad's family Ayres were well known in Reading. They had all sorts of businesses. I was Lois Ayres. Father had a greengrocer shop then took the Plough in Tilehurst. I had two sisters; Vera the eldest and Nina and two brothers, Bill and Harold, I went to Norcot School when I was little. I remember Empire Day when I asked if I could dress up as 'Canada' as my brothers were out there.

My father was the licensee of the Plough in School Road but he died at the age of 49. There was an outstanding debt to the brewers so my mother ran the pub for some time with my help in order to pay off this debt. When my brother Bill got home from Canada Mr Haddock had just built the houses in St Michael's Road and he bought her one.

When I was about eleven years old I moved on to Wilson School. We walked across the allotments to get there. We had a jolly good cook at school. The first pancake I tossed landed on the blackboard! We had a lovely cookery school in the grounds. Wilson School became a war hospital so we had to go through on the tram to Wokingham School. I sang for the wounded soldiers in the hospital during the First World War. I loved singing. I had singing lessons, four guineas a term - a lot of money on those days. My teacher used to come down from London. It was in Broad Street, the College of Music, and when my mother couldn't afford it Miss Jones said, "I won't let you give up, you can run errands and do a bit of dusting." But my mother wouldn't let me go on with it. I was seventeen when I left school, you could stay on if you wanted to. We used to go through all day, take our lunch and have it in the park. I never did go to work as I stayed home with mother, except for a few weeks in the Millinery Department at Wellsteeds.

Some of the people in Tilehurst had their own ponies and traps, they did at Westwood House.

There were stables at the Plough and the brewers made the front of the coach house into my husband's estate office. On the other side of the Plough there used to be a long garden with a little old thatched cottage at the end. I have a photo of Langley Hill with the gates halfway down. The woods are still there, Frazer's Woods, and Mr Frazer had the big house at the top. There was nothing much on the opposite side to the Plough but fields and a house which had a smithy with stable doors. Then Miss Townsend, who was Mrs Newbery's sister, turned her little bungalow into a Post Office. Nothing else, the cottages which had been on the Triangle had been pulled down. When they built the shops next to the Plough our garden went.

Dr Hosford was in School Road, he was the only one with a car. He lived halfway down and it has been turned into flats now. On the corner of Westwood Road and Armour Road there was a tennis club. There was also a tennis club in Crescent Road. The one in Westwood Road was quite nice. I was there when my brother Bill first came home from Canada. Someone said to me, "There's a gentleman looking for you with a sort of Canadian hat on!." I threw my racquet down and ran. It was my brother Bill. We walked down Westwood Road home with our arms round each other.

I was a founder member of the WI. When it started I wasn't married. I was married in 1926. There weren't many members as it was quite a small village and most of them came from the bottom of Kentwood Hill or Oaktree Road in those days.

When we had the Plough there were three bars, one of which had a spitoon and another more comfortable bar where we always had a fire. We had lamps at first, then gas. Water came from a tap but it was pumped. My mother used the laundry in Norcot Road. Apart from Baylis of Reading delivering groceries, milk was delivered by handcart. We took a jug out and it was ladled out from a churn. I remember the lamplighters but I don't think there were lamps in Tilehurst in the very early days. Then there was the muffin man who came round every Sunday carrying his tray on his head and ringing a bell. He also occasionally sold winkles. There was a rag and bone man who came from time to time as there were no dustbin collections of course. All our debris was burnt in our garden.

We had two policemen in the village. The head one lived in School Road and Mr Groves lived in Recreation Road. They had a very easy life as Tilehurst was a very law abiding community. I reckon they dealt mainly with poachers and drunks.

Both my sisters were apprentices to Wellsteeds and when they completed their training they got good jobs in London. I wanted to work and train there and worked for a month, but when the time came for my mother to sign my training agreement papers, she would not sign them. I think it was because she was afraid I would go to London as well. So I helped mother in the pub. We occasionally walked down the footpath by St Michael's Church to Tilehurst Road and across the park to hear the bands play on Sundays, and also went to the Forbury Gardens to hear the band.

The son of Mr Bull who used to own the departmental store in Broad Street was very sweet on me and was always calling, then on one occasion his friend Leslie Hedges came to Tilehurst with him and that was how our romance began.

After I was married I attended some wonderful balls at the old Town Hall. These were police balls as my father-in-law was a top ranking policeman.

I can also remember the original Prince of Wales pub. It was small and laid back with fields all around it and then there was the small golf course between Norcot Road and Water Road, now called The Links.

There were children's street parties for the 1935 Jubilee celebrations. There was one in Wendover Way; my boys went there with the Hallidays. We didn't have one in School Road.

Interviewed in February and December 1993

Delivering the beer

MR GEORGE CRITCHELL
born 1911

formerly of School Road

We moved up to Tilehurst in 1916 just before I was five to take over the old Prince of Wales pub. The old pub stood considerably nearer the road than the present one. The only food we served was bread, cheese and pickles. I remember almost half a loaf of bread with cheese and pickles cost 4d, and that was a meal. Usually these were served in the evening, for supper. The bulk of the population that I mixed with as a boy lived in Downing Road or Chapel Hill. Westwood Road was hardly developed then and there was a cluster of houses around the Little Plough. The old Triangle had a row of three or four small cottages on it and they've all gone. There were a pair of houses on the corner opposite in the road that is now blocked off but which used to carry on from Westwood Road and there were another pair virtually opposite the Little Plough. There were a pair of cottages where the road now joins what is St Michael's Road and four other cottages on the way down to the Church, which was then called Church Road. There were also two big houses; one was South Lodge and the other was The Priory and they were opposite each other. As far as I know South Lodge was not a lodge to another house, it was just a better class house.

I also remember St Mary's Orphanage which occupied a large house near the crossroads at the western end of Westwood Road. The house (with its colonial style verandah roof over the downstairs front windows) is still there almost opposite the top of Pierce's Hill. It was used as an orphanage from about 1913 to 1922. So far as I can remember the inmates were girls, and they attended Park Lane School during my time there.

Immediately adjacent to the Prince of Wales at the time we were there, there was nothing on the same side of the road between the pub and the Bath Road apart from Park Farm which lay back opposite the reservoir. Park Farm was originally the old workhouse and after the war when housing was short, somebody bought it up and ran it as a boarding house. Across the road in Park Lane was the single reservoir.

The Prince of Wales belonged to H & G Simonds in those days and their dray was either horse-drawn or later on they had a Foden steam driven lorry. We bought our bread from the bakers opposite. Next to that there were two or three more cottages in one of which 'Strap' Wickens lived. He was caretaker of Park Lane School. Then there was another pair of cottages before Westwood Road in one of which Mr Wing used the front room as a sweet shop. The present shop on the corner of Westwood Road wasn't built until about the late 1920's. Mr Winchcomb was the first owner of that. He was a newsagent and sweet shop proprietor but it's changed over the years. It's an estate agents now.

The changes to Tilehurst started with the laying of the main sewer. That was the Corporation's effort for the demobbed servicemen of the First World War. Once the sewer was installed housing development started all over the place. The first houses that I can remember, which was in the early 1920's, was the row of houses that Francis Bros put up in the then Church Road. Then in 1927 RJ Haddock bought the field behind the old Prince of Wales and put up houses in Beechwood Avenue, the first part of St Michael's Road and up to the end of his field which fronted Chapel Hill, the row of houses opposite the school. Then after that the Haddock firm expanded and continued building all the way up Park Lane from about 1930 onwards. That was virtually continuous building development and I presume it was going on all over in the rest of Tilehurst wherever there was spare land because there is hardly a plot left now. After the war when they developed The Meadway and Mayfair, everything changed dramatically.

Interviewed in November 1998

MR KEN ENGLEFIELD
born 1916

formerly of Westwood Glen and Lower Armour Road

I was born in Westwood Glen which was just a small lane with a big ditch one side about four foot deep, and the water used to run right down there across Pierce's Hill into what they called the Dene. The two old houses are still there today. There was a small lane, a pathway and up the top of there was a rabbit warren with hundreds and hundreds of rabbits.

We used to go chestnutting in Summer Woods and got chased out of there many a time by the policeman and the keeper.

We used to have a flower show once a year where the bowling green is. That was a big thing in Tilehurst back in 1925. There weren't many houses, we used to go down and sit on Tilehurst station and watch the trains go through. The ferry still ran from the Roebuck; a penny to go over the ferry in them days.

When I was a youngster there was no tarmac; the roads were all gravel, no paths as such. There was just a little hump and you walked on that. In the summer they used to have a water cart, to lay the dust, a horse and cart. It must have held two hundred gallons and he had a lever and it was like a watering can at the back. We used to run behind that in the summer and get all wet.

Later we moved to Lower Armour Road until I was married. I started work with Francis Bros in Armour Road in 1930. I was apprenticed to the plumbing. I was fourteen on the Sunday and started work on the Monday. I went round Gratwicke Road and a chappy was flashing the chimney. I went up on the ladder with him on my first day. I remember that. We built all those houses round Gratwicke Road,

Thicket Road and Bramble Crescent. They were built in 1930. I finished at Francis Bros in 1954.

My son doesn't believe me, but when I worked at Yattendon I had to bike there night and morning with my tools, not many kids would do it now. We used to start at eight until half past four in the winter and half past five in the summer, an hour for dinner. In the winter we only had a half hour for dinner. Saturday mornings it was eight to twelve. My first week's wages as an apprentice were 7/6d (37.5p) I can remember it as if it were yesterday. I give it to my Mum and she give me threepence back. When you think about it we were born too soon. I started smoking when I was fourteen, a packet of Woodbines was twopence. A tradesman was paid £2.10s a week. That was good money in them days. Our Dad was a lorry driver on Francis and he got £2 a week.

I can remember coming up Norcot Road. If you were sat on the top of the bus and you didn't watch out there was trees overhanging and you had to duck down or you would get your head knocked off! The road was all twisty. Just past the cemetery there used to be Minchin's Farm and when Francis were building the houses in 1931 or 1932 they were digging down for the sewer pipes and they found the old road about six feet underneath. Bert Wickens, he used to keep a farm ('Strappy' Wickens they used to call him) he used to do all the sewer pipes on Francis.

Do you remember when the plane crashed there, a Canadian one? The plane crashed on the bucket thing*. The buckets were built on pylons, with a net underneath where they crossed Norcot Road to stop the clay falling off on the road.

We did a lot of work down Collier's kiln, Water Road. Old Francis, when he had nearly finished his time took over Colliers. He was one of the directors and we did a lot of work there. Well we used to have a wander around during dinner breaks and we saw the buckets come over, they were massive buckets. They held about five hundredweight of clay. You could get three or four people in there and we see them tipping out and it run through great rollers to get all the impurities out, all the stones and that.

* *The buckets carried clay from the pits where Upcroft School is now, over Norcot Road to Collier's Potteries in Water Road.*

We have been in there watching them making flowerpots on a wheel. Lovely! Reg Whichelo used to be a good flowerpot maker, he used to do chimney pots as well. His old wheel would be going around and round and up it would go. A work of art you know that was.

Francis Bros used to get a lot of their bricks from Wells kilns, you know where the fever hospital used to be? The chimney stood until recently (by the Meadway Precinct). He used to get a lot of his stuff there, his bricks, but the majority of his stuff came from Colliers.

They had three lorry drivers on Francis; Mr Mandrell, Mr Pocock and my dad. Petrol lorries they was, Fords. The first one he drove had no windscreen, in the rain they put a sheet up. No side window, he used to get wet! A lot of the timber came from Warwicks and from Ridleys in King's Road. Right opposite where the Shop on the Bridge used to be, there was a little side road where Ridleys were. I used to see them cut the wood on a circular saw.

How much do you think I paid for my first bicycle? Four pound nineteen and six; that was a Hercules. I remember when Newbery Park wasn't a park. It was full of gorse bushes, thick as anything. We used to go and play football over there, we wasn't supposed to, but we did.

Interviewed in September 1995

The barrel organ came round every Monday

MRS JOAN MARTIN
born 1923

formerly of Blundells Road

I came to Tilehurst in 1926 when I was three. My grandparents lived here and my parents came to live in Reading because my grandmother was far from well. Dad got a job with Sewards the baker in Norcot Road, which then went on to become Rules. Dad used to get up early in the morning to 'punch' the dough, as he called it, then he would go out with the horse and cart to deliver the bread.

I was five and went to Park Lane School and stayed until I was eleven and we used to have to go to bed in the afternoons. I ended up in Miss Wheeler's class and I loved it. She also taught my daughter.

On Mondays when mother did the washing there used to be an old man with a barrel organ who came to the bottom of Blundells Road and played, and mother used to give me a penny and say, "Go and give it to the gentleman and come straight back into the garden." He seemed old to me then. I can't remember whether he had a monkey.

We lived in Gratwicke Road; there were two houses going from Blundells Road and we lived in the second one and the rest of it was fields with cows until you got almost to the top of Gratwicke Road. There were several houses on the side of the field and just a few private houses on the other side, the rest was Blundells Woods. I spent many years in there tearing my clothes and getting a smack.

I went to Norcot School after Park Lane because in the meantime my father was put off by Rules the baker. When Seward died and Rules took over they had a van and father couldn't drive. (Father's name was Bonnett). So Dad was put off. My grandmother died and this left my grandfather in the house in Polstead Road. He was my mother's father, his name was Long, and my mother said, "I can't keep two houses going." So we had to live in Polstead Road. My mother had a tough time I can tell you. My grandfather had a stroke and I was 12 or 13 and had to do a lot to help my mother. She had to wash, feed him, everything. He never came out of the bedroom. You didn't get any help in those days. Anyway, I expect it gives you a backbone. Mother was a good Christian woman. No nonsense.

Dad used to get weekend work at Parslows and that sort of thing and glad of it, but when the war came he went to the Co-op bakery in Grovelands Road. He lived to be 82 and Mum lived to be 93 but it was hard on my parents; I have an easy life in comparison. The Co-op bakery started using horses in the wartime.

In Recreation Road there was a lady who had a shop that sold all sorts of things. Her name was Butterworth and she had a little grocery shop in her front room. I know my mother always went there as she never went to the Co-op - she wouldn't have become a 'Co-oper' if my Dad hadn't got a job at the bakery and you had to belong. Mother used to like the little shops. Although they always had a slate Mother never had anything unless she could pay for it. What you couldn't afford you went without. You saved up until you had the money.

When we were living in Polstead Road my father had been on the dole for so long that in those days they gave you a ticket to go to Tesco in Union Street. My mother tore it up, she would not accept it. She would rather go out and scrub somebody's house or floor and get half a crown a morning. She took in washing; she used to do washing for Mrs Bryant - her sheets - and wrapped them in brown paper and I had to carry them carefully so as not to crease them. She also grew things in the garden. Now when we went to Polstead Road grandfather had an allotment down there and he kept a pig; I can remember we used to keep all the peelings and things. We had 1cwt of coal at Christmas from Tilehurst Poor Lands - Mr Illsley was the Treasurer. Now mother accepted that because everybody had the same.

When I left Norcot School I went to evening classes and paid five bob, as I wanted to learn. My father was always interested in books, and we had a library down by Newbery Park. I remember getting enrolled and Dad used to pick out these books for me - I think I read every classic in the library. He was always interested in history and mother used to read to me as a child, so I have always been interested in books.

When I first started work my father said I could have this bicycle which was a Raleigh and in 1941 it cost £7.2s.6d. My mother bought it but I had to repay half a crown a week. I was told to dismount by the Pond House and walk over the tramlines. I got caught in them twice! I worked at Milwards, the shoe shop, then during the war I had to go out to the place at Theale making bullets. I wanted to go into the Forces but my brother said, "You're not going in any Forces!" So I went into munitions making bullets and hated it. Sometimes I went by train from Reading West Station to Theale and sometimes I rode my bicycle. Then I went to Pulsometer and I got dust on my chest and they thought I had TB. I was working filing the burrs off the pumps to go into submarines. I remember the Duchess of Kent came round to see us, she was lovely. The men came out of there black, filthy and Dr McCormick from School Road said I had to come out of there; I didn't have TB but I had about 18 months off work.

Darmody's at the end of Blundells Road had a little sweet shop. We used to go in the front room and buy a halfpenny worth of sweets. Then it got bigger and she had that little place built in her garden. She made all the sweets. Mrs Springall was down near Park Lane School and sold vegetables and one side and sweets on the other in her shop. We used to take our halfpennies in there on our way to school, and all those lovely sweets we used to buy that you only read about now. Next to Mrs Springall was the Undertaker, a Mr Gardiner. He made the coffins. We had quite a number of little shops up here including Barefoot's the cycle shop. Mr Barefoot and Mr Nuffield of Cowley started up at the same time. Barefoot stayed as he was but Nuffield went on and he became a millionaire. Miss Bowles, the nurse, lived in Kentwood Hill. She used to have a 'sit up and beg' bike and wear a funny little hat with ribbons tied under her chin.

A friend and myself used to walk down Pierce's Hill and get chestnuts from the Lord of the Manor's trees which hung over the road. (Westwood House)

I remember when they gave us the park, Newbery Park. I thought that was wonderful; we spent hours over there. We always had park keepers. Up in the rec' at Armour Road you had a park keeper and you did as you were told; he would have no nonsense. His name was Buckland and he lived in Polstead Road. He wore a peaked cap.

Now when we bought this house and we got our deeds that was very interesting to me, it's on there "Poor Lands".

When my daughter was young we walked through the woods by the Bear Inn down through that lovely bluebell wood and came out by the caravan site. Then we walked up to the farm to see the cows being milked.

Now there was a lovely old house on this estate (Park Farm House) and it was pulled down and a children's home was built. Now that has been pulled down and they are building fifteen houses. There were two wells there which they are having to fill in. Tilehurst is very much water and clay. When you come up the main road and get off the bus (Park Lane) you can walk through to where the old house was - it used to be a private lane with trees on either side.

I can remember them altering the White House corner as there was always accidents. Dr Lyn Jones had part of his garden taken. They couldn't do anything with Marshall's but they took a piece off the 'rec' and they did something to the pub corner.

Interviewed in May 1998

MRS MAVIS BEAKHOUSE
born 1920

St Michael's Road (previously Church Road)

My first memory of Tilehurst was somebody saying, 'Let's have some fish and chips!' and his mother said, "You will have to go near the White House as they are the only ones who cook their fish in solid fat." I can still see those great big boxes of fat; somebody said not to lean up against them or we'd get all the fat over us.

There's one little thing that I have not seen mentioned in all the books on Tilehurst, and I have read them all, and that was tithe charges. There was a tithe on the land where our house was built. The charge was 3d a half year but the Tithe Redemption Committee, who applied the charge, liked it to be paid annually - ie 6d. There was an opportunity to make a one-off payment of 14s 6d to buy it outright. I still have the receipt.

Our house in St Michael's Road was next door to the Priory, a large house with extensive gardens and two ponds with a footpath going through the centre. Dr and Mrs Fosbury lived at the Priory for a while and she used to go out on the pond in a boat and collect duck eggs. She came up to the house one day and said she couldn't find any eggs and my husband told her to put her hand in the water beside the nest as they had probably rolled off. She found loads of them.

Then of course there was the ditch that ran along the front of our house up to the Priory and then went under the road and I assume it went on down the Moors. When they had all the floods in Reading years ago and they came round collecting for flood victims, my neighbour (he was a schoolteacher) said, "I hope you haven't been round next door as the ponds have overflowed and come right across their back garden." They couldn't see this from the front.

I saw Mayfair go up and the Meadway. We always walked into town when my son was smaller as you couldn't get pushchairs in wartime and the pram I had was too big to go on a bus. We had to go through the churchyard and back behind Ranikhet camp; there was a rough footpath which brought you down to Water Road.

You know all about the Little Plough and the two thatched cottages that were at the top. But I can't remember anybody mentioning that there was a tiny cottage right by the side. The lady there always comes to my mind, she had her hair in a bun and a white pinafore and she came out of her front door and practically walked onto the road; there was no footpath. It could only have been one up, one down. Where St Michael's Road houses start now, this one would have been right in front of the first house, to get to their house they had to go behind this little one. They took it down when the Little Plough and the others went. Why did they take them down? They were beautiful. Kate Lovegrove in the Little Plough was a lovely person.

My husband lived in Water Road and we used to go in his mother's front room and watch the horses in the kiln opposite where the buckets started and finished. His uncle was a well known character in Reading, his Uncle Bert, he worked for the Thames Conservancy. He was a real country man. He used to have a punt down at the Roebuck, you could store it there by the river.

Of course, all the houses round us weren't there when we came; you could walk out of the back garden straight into Halls Road. We used to go up City Road to the open fields up there, looking for mushrooms.

The kiln down Kentwood Hill they all mention it when Tate & Lyle had it for sugar and it caught fire, but nobody ever mentioned that after the fire they made syrup tins there. I know that's true as I worked there. The tin came in oblongs and we did the rolling and the ringing and then sent them off. During the war if you didn't have any commitments, children etc you had to go to work. I registered and they sent me there; you didn't get any free tins of syrup. Then a little bit further down there was a chicken farm. We kept some chickens in the back garden, we liked the eggs but when the poor chickens got old we didn't know what to do with them. The first one we had, we had a neighbour who came from Bucklebury who did the chicken and we got it on the table and my son said, "Mum, is that Gilly?" and we couldn't eat it!

Interviewed in June 1998

"Is that Gilly?"

Telephone:— *Telegrams:—*
CLERKENWELL 8331. TRECOM, FINSQUARE, LONDON

TITHE REDEMPTION COMMISSION.

To avoid delay, address all communications to:—
THE SECRETARY.

FINSBURY SQUARE HOUSE,
33-37, FINSBURY SQUARE,
LONDON, E.C.2.

TEMPORARY RECEIPT

Date 16 JUN 1947

Reference 3/132 / 563 K

REDEMPTION OF ANNUITIES CHARGED UNDER THE TITHE ACT, 1936.

Received the sum of .... pounds
.... Fourteen .... shillings and .... Six .... pence

A full receipt with detailed particulars will be forwarded later.

Addressee as overleaf.

FORM 509.

8/46 M21203 JC&S 1/47 702

Tithe Redemption Certificate

MR DENNIS GILL
born 1927

formerly of Wendover Way

We moved into Wendover Way which had only just been built when I was three in about 1930. My father reminded me once that when we first moved in there were only railwaymen and commercial travellers who lived there for some strange reason. My father was a goods traffic controller on the Western Railway. He worked in an office with a bank of telephones and switches. It was fascinating to see it all working. He assembled trains of goods and then routed them through. It was quite interesting.

My father always enjoyed Tilehurst. He had an allotment and was always in the Little Plough. I remember there used to be a grey parrot in there and it had a horrible whistle and made odd remarks to people, some of which were not very polite! It was a beautiful parrot. The pubs are so different now. I remember the old Prince of Wales before the present one was built. It was a white building and it had a big clapboard fence all the way round the outside of it. It was rebuilt at the same time as the Bear Inn. They are very similar in style. I think that was about 1936 or thereabouts. The Bear Inn was built when the trolley buses were extended up to the top of Tilehurst .

My mother was quite a character. Laura Gill founded the Darby and Joan Club in Tilehurst. She ran it in the Village Hall in Victoria Road although she had wanted to run it in the Methodist Hall but she couldn't get it. It distressed her that the Village Hall was so far away from everybody. She only died in 1997, she was 99.

I went to Park Lane school first of all and then after the 10-plus I went to Wilson Central School and left at 14 and went to sea when I was 15. I remember a photograph being taken of the boys who passed the exam. The boys at the back went to Wilson and the boys in front passed to go to Reading Grammar. It was a kind of farewell picture. I remember the teacher Miss Wheeler, she took the top class. She had a great friend, Miss Jordan, and they were never apart. Miss Jordan took the class about two years below Miss Wheeler. My daughter went to Park Lane for about six months when we were between houses and were staying with my mother in Wendover Way and Miss Wheeler and Miss Jordan were still there! I went round the school last year. It was the first time I'd been back since I left in 1938. The hall was not cluttered in our day as it is now; it used to be empty and we used to have races in there. We used to race three abreast from one end of the hall to the other. The Headteacher was Miss Ferris.

We were moved around during the War; we went to some little halls. There was Elm Park Hall and another at the bottom of Wilson Road. We went to Wilson School in 1938 and weren't evacuated from there until 1940. It became a war hospital, not for serious injuries.

I remember the air raid shelter at the Triangle - it was for the wardens. When the war was over they sealed it up and covered it over. The only other shelters I remember were in Downing Road. They were fairly sturdy buildings on the road, not underground.

I remember as a child going to a garden party at the Priory and taking out a rowing boat on the ponds. Dr Fosbury owned it then. His father had owned it before him. Young Dr Fosbury started the surgery up at Westwood Road on the corner there and now I believe the practice has gone down Norcot Hill.

There was a guy who we called Bungalow Jack. He kept pheasants and we used to steal his eggs. Imagine coming out of Wendover Way and turning right. You carried on up Church Road which at that time linked up with Halls Road which then bore left and then right to go up to the Church and the Rectory (Iris Court). On that actual corner was the area of Bungalow Jack's ground. He had quite a lot of ground and we'd climb over the fence and sneak around with great fear and pinch these eggs. We didn't dare take them home because we'd get into trouble so we boiled them in tin cans. Nowadays we'd be called hooligans!

There was an interesting character called Abery whose daughter used to run the Little Plough and who lived in the thatched cottages by the pub. This guy used to work at Water Road where the buckets came. He walked from his cottage to Water Road every morning. He had these old corduroy moleskin trousers with a strap round and a carpet bag with a bottle of tea in. I remember when we came back home on leave, there were several of us in uniform, we'd get into the Little Plough and he was there. He'd always manage to empty his glass just as we got up!

Of course in those days people were less mobile and so we spent most of our time in the village. But when we were kids we'd go down on our cycles to the River Kennet down the Burghfield Road and we'd swim there. Sometimes we'd explore and end up towards Whitley and we'd begin to get a bit nervous as they were all strangers there. So you see we were fairly well restricted to our own area. We knew our own people pretty well. In fact my wife came from the Katesgrove area and she didn't know anyone from this part. She used to say that the 'nobs' lived here!

I learned to swim at a place we called 'The Tum'. You went down Langley Hill and at the bottom you followed a lane, through where the big estate is now, and this took you down to the Holybrook and the Kennet. It was muddy and slimy but that was the sort of place you swam in the 30's.

As boys we had gangs and we were the Church Road Gang. There was Frank Hemmings, Donald White (who lives in Brighton now), Mike Jessup, Les Howard (now living in Canada) and myself. We used to play football on a bit of spare ground which was the link between Church Road and Blundells Road, you know where Blundells Copse is. It was near Bungalow Jack's ground. You'd hear him shouting at us! He was not very friendly to kids who were invading his property!

In Church Road was another guy who was older than us. The bungalow that his mother had is still there very nearly opposite where the Priory used to be. His name was Walter Brooks and he occasionally used to come across to the tennis club in Woodlands Drive. He joined the Air Force pre-war and became a Squadron Leader and he used to come and beat Tilehurst up in this Hawker Hart which was a biplane fighter before the war started. He'd drop little parachutes out with messages to his mother! Of course, it was fairly unusual to see a plane in those days. We always knew it was him because his mum used to come out and wave to him!

We used to walk down a little lane that went alongside his property to get to my father's allotment which is how we knew of him. He was quite a well-known personality around the place at the time. He was killed in the Battle of Britain.

Our family all belonged to Woodlands Tennis Club. Very few people in the club lived outside Wendover Way and Woodlands Drive. Now I understand that hardly anyone from that area actually plays tennis there. I went to the tennis club recently and it was very different. It now has two hard courts whereas we used to have three grass courts and it's a bit run down. But when we were young it was *the* place, the focal point of the area. R J Haddock built quite a lot of houses round the area; he built Wendover Way, Woodlands Drive and Beechwood Avenue, then he built the Southcote estate and over at Emmer Green. He put a tennis club in each estate and we used to play for the RJ Haddock Cup. They would all come over from Southcote to Woodlands and compete with each other. Beechwood Avenue had a club as well, but they eventually built a house in it. The standard was fairly good, although none of us was going to Wimbledon and in fact my sister became County standard and played quite determinedly eventually. We were all members; we juniors were taught to play by the seniors. I suppose it was a bit snobbish in a way. Tennis is snobbish, they don't like the 'hoi polloi', which is perhaps why as a nation we are not as good as we ought to be! But we all played, even my mother. She was a right rabbit, she couldn't hit the ball over the net!

Woodlands Tennis Club was originally a school. Jack Wynn the builder went there.

I started working at McIlroy's in 1949 when I left the sea. At that time Mr McIlroy wasn't there as they had been taken over by then by Gossard. They only owned it for a very short while and then it was bought by Courtaulds.

I was a trainee buyer, which was another name for a skivvy! They called the building the Reading Crystal Palace. It was very inspiring, but it never made any money. It just wasn't workable. There were loads of demobbed servicemen working there. It was a barn-like place with very old fixtures, very much over-staffed and had too much space. At that period there were four department stores in the town; Heelas, Bulls, McIlroys and Wellsteeds.

There was a side entrance in West Street but the main entrance was in Oxford Street. There was a roller-skating rink in Palmer Hall which was in West Street. When I worked at McIlroys it was very difficult to get houses, you couldn't even get a licence to build a house, so people rented rooms. We had rooms in Chatham Street for about six/seven weeks and then I got an opportunity to get a flat above McIlroys because staff used to live in. It was on the very top floor, you can just see the windows there now. There were living-in staff. Not many - a couple of dozen maybe with a house-mother who was no better than she should have been! And as part of my deal of having this flat with free electricity I had to go in every fortnight on Sunday morning from six o'clock to eight o'clock to relieve Mr Prior, the nightwatchman, until the daywatchman came on.

I remember a funny story about the Priory which used to be in Church Road. Many years later when my career had taken off and I was doing some business in Hong Kong, I was lying in my hotel bedroom reading the paper and there was a snippet from Reuters reporting a plague of frogs in Church Road!

Interviewed in July 1998

Logs from Jerome

GEORGE BURGESS
born 1921

I was born in 1921 at 12 Church Road, Tilehurst. I went to school at Park Lane and then went to Norcot when I was about eleven years old.

The cottage in Church Road had two rooms. There was a front room and then a scullery; it had a tiled floor and a wooden staircase went up one side. There were two bedrooms and a garden where we used to keep chickens and grow vegetables. There was a large shed and the bucket toilet was in there. My father used to get up about four o'clock in the morning and dig a hole at the bottom of the garden and empty the bucket.

My father went to the National School - 1/6d a week I think - a small fee had to be paid. My father lived in Church Road. The old grandfather was a lot older than my grandmother, they ran the laundry. He was married first to a Boseley from Calcot. I can't remember him at all as he died when my father was thirteen years old. He had a horse and cart and one day when he was delivering washing down to Brunswick Street it was icy and the horse slipped and ran over his feet, which started his problems.

Going down Church Road past the Little Plough there were two cottages. My granny Meredith lived in one and people called Butlins in the other. There is a row of newish houses down there built in the 1930's and those two old cottages stood right in front of them.

St Michael's Road used to be all fields and I have been told that the old granny used to go over there. Apparently when the rabbits have young they make a hole, and granny used to put her hand down the hole, get the rabbits and cook them!

The Little Plough was opposite our cottage in Church Road. It was a funny little place really. You used to go in the gateway down a step into the bar and there was another bar round the corner. Outside there were some old sheds where they had forms and tables and when people were out walking on a Sunday evening they called in for a drink and sat out there with the children.

We moved to Bramble Crescent in 1935. We used to go and play down in the woods. Down the bottom was what they called the Withies, that was very wet and lovely kingcups and flags and stuff like that grew there. But coming back up to Bramble Crescent there was a gravel pit. It used to fill up with water and rubbish was dumped there. There used to be a plain that wasn't flooded and we went there playing tick tack.

We had a bonfire occasionally and brought potatoes from home; this was in the woods at the bottom of Thicket Road. One of the Dibleys brought an accordion and we had a sing-song and these jacket potatoes. There were about fifteen to twenty of us I suppose. Of course we used to climb trees and make camps and all that sort of thing. We got in fights, but friendly sort of fights, you know.

I remember they came to the Plough selling rabbits at 6d a time and you used to get 2d off the rag and bone man for the skins. The rag and bone man came round the streets and there used to be an old boy from Calcot to sweep the chimneys. There was a fishmonger who came round the streets. He came from Calcot - Wedlock, I think. He always used to stop outside the Little Plough with his pushcart and go in and have a drink. I think the butcher Wedlock in School Road was a relation.

Timmer's rose nursery used to be on the corner of Churchend Lane, then it was turned into a caravan site. One of the Cooper's sons had that. They had Fox Farm down the corner of Church Road and Cockney Hill. On Saturdays I took the greengrocery out for Marshalls and sometimes I went down to Coopers with a big sack and filled it with cabbages from the fields for 6d or something ridiculous like that, took them back to the shop and that was what they used to trade on.

I remember Miss Ferris and Miss Goodyear at Park Lane School. Miss Goodyear's father was a sidesman at St Michael's

Church. I was in the choir there, we went to the National School for choir practice. I think we used to get something like 1/6d for weddings. I know we got into a lot of trouble because down Church Road, about 200 yards past Woodlands Drive they had a big privet hedge and we used to run from one side of the road to the other and jump this hedge. We were reported to the Church.

The cottages down Downing Road are old and there used to be a man called Jerome who had a wood business and came round with logs. He had a horse and cart and brought the logs round in old wicker baskets. There was a lady by the name of Parr who kept the Royal Oak. You went down the bottom of Downing Road (the farm there was owned by Wickens), down a footpath over a little stream, it had a small wooden bridge, and you came up by the Royal Oak. There were some cottages there and one family was called Hazell. There were some more Hazells down Downing Road who bred canaries. There were two old boys living in the cottages at the back of Downing Road, Teddy Brocks and his brother. Somebody by the name of Abery had the Little Plough at the end and she married a Lovegrove.

Interviewed in October 1993

4th Form at Park Lane School 1955

RICHARD BEAKHOUSE
born 1945

formerly of St Michael's Road (previously Church Road)

I was born in Dellwood which was down by Prospect Park in Liebenrood Road and as a child I lived in St Michael's Road right next to the house which used to be The Priory which is now Keswick Close. That was before they built Corwen Road and at that time the Meadway only came down as far as the end of St Michael's Road. I had a grandmother who lived in Water Road down near Prospect Park. My parents came from Kent and moved to Tilehurst a couple of years before I was born in 1945.

A few doors up from me was a family called the Champions. I called them Aunt and Uncle although they weren't, but in those days everyone called their neighbours Aunt and Uncle. They owned some land down St Michael's Road and the entrance to their land is the alleyway that joins St Michael's Road and Corwen Road. You could go down there and they owned some fields which went from there across to Blundells Copse. That was compulsorily purchased by the Council in 1955/6. In Blundells Copse there was an old pit where we would go and catch newts. That pond was used as a general rubbish dump and was filled with all sorts of old scrap iron. Builders used to dump their rubbish in it but you could always catch newts there, despite the fact that it was all polluted.

There was old Mr and Mrs Champion and then there was Bill and Alice who were their children. It was Alice and Bill who I called Aunt and Uncle. I can't really remember old Mr and Mrs Champion. Alice was known as Bubbles. Bill worked first of all for the railway and then he used to keep a few pigs and chickens and grow some corn on that patch of land. I can remember as kids we would go up there and ask him for jobs to do and he would give us some odd jobs and he'd pay us by giving us an egg. We'd come home with an egg and we thought this was wonderful. On his plot of land there was a railway carriage which had First and Second Class on it. A father and son who were a bit like Steptoe and Son lived in this railway carriage and they had a horse and cart and a rag and bone business. It was a brown carriage, I think it was a Great Western one. When we used to talk to Bill he'd say it was the only way those two would ever have first class living accommodation! One day these two old boys who lived in the railway carriage moved some neighbours of ours with their horse and cart up to the pre-fabs at the top of Mayfair. I remember my friend and I helped to load the cart and walked behind it and then helped to unload the furniture when we got there. A horse and cart was not such an unusual a sight in and around Tilehurst in the late 1950's and early 1960's. They were still quite common. Bill Champ' used to keep pigs and he always used a horse and cart to go to the cattle market on a Saturday morning. My friend Glennie and I would go with him and on the way back we'd call in at the butchers and the odd cafe, and we'd pick up their bins of swill. By the time we got to Norcot Hill the cart was too loaded to carry us all so we would walk up by the side of the horse. When we got to the 'yard' as he called it we would tip all the bones and food slops into a big galvanised water tank and then boil it up by putting a load of car tyres underneath and that would feed the pigs for the week. Everyone used to say how nice the bacon tasted!

When their land was compulsorily purchased, the Champions moved out to Rag Hill at Aldermaston. When Bill first moved out there he still used the horse and cart to go backwards and forwards to Reading market. This was in the late 1950's.

I started with Francis Bros the builders in Tilehurst in 1962 - Corwen Road had been put through by then but we built some of the flats and council houses along there.

When I was a kid the Meadway stopped at the end of St Michael's Road and you could go from St Michael's Road down past the church. To get to my grandmother's house in Water Road we would go down behind St Michael's church where there was a footpath that used to come out round about where the Meadway meets Dee

Road. You would go up and over the top and down Dee Road which was just a footpath then. That was before they built any of the houses on the Dee Road Estate. As kids we would play in the old clay pits at the back of Water Road. There were brick kilns either side of Water Road and the ones on the Tilehurst side closed down first. They were empty for years and we used to go and play over there in the old building. The big chimneys that used to be for the brick kiln had long brick tunnels going to the ovens. It always used to be the dare to see who would go along this tunnel and look up the chimney.

They used to dig the clay where the Potteries estate is now and the buckets went overhead to more or less where the fire station is now and the clay was unloaded to weather there for a year. Then it was loaded into buckets again and it would go overhead to the kiln in Water Road. After it had been weathered it used to come up through some woods in Dee Road and there were allotments there. We would go up into the woods and the buckets would come along very low, near the ground and the idea was to hang onto these buckets and see who could hang on longest before you dropped!

In the mid to late 1950's the Army used to practise shooting in the sand pits on the Tilehurst side of Water Road and as kids we would lay on top of the pit and watch them doing their practice. As soon as they had gone, if you were down there quick, you could pick up the old cartridge cases. I remember one day we found this one complete bullet and rushed back to my grandmother's house, put the bullet in a vice and we were just there with the pliers trying to get the bullet open when my Dad came in! Fortunately he stopped us just in time!

The Army blew up the chimneys which were at the back of Water Road. We all looked out of the bedroom windows and they blew these chimney stacks up. We watched them all drop, one after the other. The kiln there was empty for a long time.

There was a sand pit where Upton Road is now, just off Dee Road and all the face of the pit was holes and there were lots of sand-martins. However, over on the other side, the Norcot side, it was clay pits.

Francis Bros was linked family-wise with Colliers and still had some involvement with them. When I joined them they were an old local building contractor and funeral parlour. In those days most of the old builders used to do undertaking as well. They had the joiners shop at the back of the premises and the joiners would have the bodies laid out on the bench while they made up the coffins. With the window and door frames, they'd run up a few coffins! They'd stopped that by the time I joined in 1962!

I remember there was a fish and chip shop at The Triangle, in the parade of shops where the chemist is now. There has always been one at the top of Norcot Road, but the one at the Triangle closed down quite early on. In the centre of the Triangle used to be the old air raid shelters. In fact I think they are still there under the mounds. All they did was concrete over the sloping doors into the shelters. We would sit on top of them eating our chips. My father used to work in Feltham in Middlesex and he never got home until seven o'clock at night. When it was Bonfire Night my mate and I would wait for him on top of the shelters to rush him home to get the bonfire lit! We would sit eating our chips conning people for a penny for the Guy!

Over the road where Kentucky Fried Chicken is now used to be the Post Office which was a bungalow. The woman in there was a typical postmistress; she had her hair pulled back in a tight bun, a very strict woman. In those days you could buy sixpenny savings stamps and I used to go with in with my savings book. Then there was Breretons the ironmongers opposite the Prince of Wales pub. He used to have a van come round selling paraffin. It was this chap's son who was the policeman killed at Hungerford in that terrible shooting. I was at Park Lane school with him.

When I started school you did one year at Park Lane and then two or three years down at the Laurels and then back up to Park Lane school. In my last year at Park Lane, Norcot became another junior school. It used to be a senior school, but when Stoneham was built, everybody went there and they split Park Lane and people went to Norcot as the junior school. Park Lane had been given a bit of land the year before at the end of Downing Road for a playing field. Before that we just used the playground. I remember we had the same teachers all the way through the school. One year we'd have Miss Wheeler and the next Miss Jordan and they would alternate as we went on through the school. We had 48 in the class, in four rows of twelve, and you sat in order depending on where you were in the class. There was no being careful with people's feelings. Miss Clamp was the headmistress, then there was Miss Wheeler, Miss Jordan, Mr Channing (who was my next-door-neighbour), Mr Wiles (super teacher he was) and Mrs Fisher (she used to live in St Michael's Road too and was a very strict teacher). I remember at playtimes we used to rub ha'pennies on the stone window ledges to smooth the faces off and one day we had a lecture telling us it was illegal to do that! And another lecture we got was when Ranikhet camp was empty. There were all these old timber buildings that were empty and we would go and play in them as kids. I remember a couple of the lads started pulling the timber off to go and make themselves a shed at home and the policeman caught them. The following morning in school assembly Miss Clamp stood up and said that these two boys were going to be taken to court for stealing timber and how wrong it was. We were all trembling thinking we were going to get into trouble too.

School swimming lessons used to be down at Coley near Berkeley Avenue. There was a swimming bath there which was fed from the Holybrook. It was an open air pool and we used public transport to get there. I remember one day in particular when we were to be tested. Those who could swim a width got a certificate. As usual the water was green, you couldn't see the bottom. We were all made to stand along the side in the water and then this very strict woman came along and said, "Now, you swim across!" The poor devils at the end of this line of 48 children were getting really cold. Then I saw a frog swim past me and the girl next to me saw it too and went into hysterics over it! We couldn't get the girl back in the pool and all she had to do was swim a width!

We used to cycle down there in the evenings and we would take the valves out of your tyres because other people would take them out otherwise as a joke! You had to take them into the changing room with you and pump your tyres up again to cycle home! Our other favourite swimming spot was down at the lido in Scour's Lane. There was a changing room on the river bank, a grassed area, and there were these white horizontal poles that fenced it off and a springboard. It was lovely in the summer. If a launch came along pulling a dinghy at the back they used to shout out "Tender!" and all the lads would jump in and swim out and hang on the back of this boat to see who could go farthest up the river. But I've seen some of the launch owners hitting the boys with their oars to try and stop them hanging on the back of the boat. I think it cost 6d to change there, but again you didn't dare leave your towel in the room, so you'd take your towel and your clothes back out to the bank. There was always a rough element down there who might kick your clothes into the water and you'd have to go home wet! We used to ask Bill Champ' if he had any old lorry inner tubes and we'd take them down to the garage near Scour's Lane to get them pumped up to use as rubber rings.

We used to go fishing along there too. In those days you didn't need a licence - it was free all along that stretch of the Thames. Sometimes we went along the Kennet where the Cunning Man is and fish along there. Some of the lads used to go swimming down at Monk Yard but it was a bit dangerous there.

I went to Alfred Sutton senior school. I took the 11-plus. If you passed really well you went to Reading School or there was Stoneham Grammar. After that it was a choice between Alfred Sutton, Ashmead and EP Collier, depending on what you wanted to do. If you wanted to go into building you'd go to Ashmead. If you failed the 11-plus initially you went to Norcot and then later it would be Stoneham Secondary Modern. Alfred Sutton was one of the first comprehensives. When I went, there was grammar stream and two 'modern' classes. It worked quite well in those days as you could transfer from one to the other. A couple of lads got dropped from the selective stream because they were not coping with the lessons and another couple got moved up from the modern stream and they just about coped. So despite what they say, the 11-plus seemed to work. When I was at Park Lane and it came to the 11-plus it was a really big thing. Parents and teachers were both on to you to do well. I remember there was another exam we had to sit called the Murray House which was to see whether you could sit the 11-plus! There was some big boxing match on one night in the States and I remember sitting up until 3 o'clock in the morning listening to the fight with my dad. The next morning I was really tired and we had the Murray House test and I got a lecture from Miss Wheeler about looking tired. In those days parents didn't have any involvement at all in the school. Most of the female teachers were unmarried, we had dipped pens right the way up, spellings, chanting the tables and marks for handwriting. Despite having 48 in a class it seemed to work, although I can remember Miss Wheeler standing there and saying, "You've all got the same size brains, so you should all be able to do it!" which they wouldn't say now, of course. They were quite good, the teachers. If they said, "Be quiet!" you were quiet! And in the playground in the morning when the whistle was blown we all had to stand still and be quiet before we went in. They had that kind of authority.

My mother lived next door to the Priory which was a house with two big lakes in the grounds. In the winter we would knock on the door and ask if we could skate on the ice. One year a lad fell through and my dad heard him crying for help and he laid some ladders across the ice to get him out. It wasn't deep enough for him to drown, but of course it was freezing cold. It was built on in about 1964 and they dug the silt out of the lakes and filled them in. We always had a lot of frogs, but that year there was a plague of them because they had nowhere to go. It even made the national papers! The roads were covered with squashed frogs. When we cut our grass that year we had to wear wellingtons. We had a long back garden and a rotary mower and you couldn't see always see the frogs in the grass! There were thousands of them. My mother still gets hundreds of frogs go to her fishpond every year. We scoop the spawn out and chuck it on the compost heap, but they still come back every year. But that first year they were laying their eggs in any patch of damp they could find. We never realised how many frogs went to those ponds.

The old house was quite a big house, but I never knew why it was called The Priory. At one time Dr Fosbury used to live there, then it went through two or three different people then they sold it on and Browns the builders from Armour Road developed it.

When they started building the houses in the Meadway there was a great uproar about what they should call it. People didn't want it to be called Mayfair, because Mayfair was the council houses - snobbery really - so they called it the Meadway. The people who lived between the end of St Michael's Road (which was originally Church Road) and Mayfair wanted their bit of road to be called Hall's Road, but it became part of the Meadway. There was quite a hoo-hah about it at the time.

I remember visiting my grandfather when he was in Blagrave Hospital. You could wheel the patients out onto the verandah. It was a lovely spot. I remember it as being a convalescent hospital. We used to take my grandfather eggs. If you took an egg in they would write the patient's name on it and they could have a boiled egg for tea! We used to play in that neck of the woods, around City Road. When I was at school I did a paper round from Park Lane up round City Road.

I remember the Little Plough pub before it was pulled down. We used to go there as kids. They had a tin shed in the garden with a bench and a table. Not that my parents went to the pub much! But my mate's parents did and we used to have a Pepsi Cola and a packet of crisps. That was when we first tried vinegar on crisps. You could only ever get plain crisps with a little blue twist of paper with salt in. Somebody came up with the idea of putting vinegar in and shaking the bag up. In those days the beer bottle tops were crimped, like they are now, but they used to have a bit thick piece of cork in the back of them to seal them on. You could get this piece of cork out and if you put it on your shirt you could press it back in and it would hold like a badge. My mate came up with the idea that we could make a suit of armour. So we went up there three days running to see Aunty Kate, the landlady, and asked her for all her beer bottle tops. So she gave us a big bag of bottle tops and we took them home and we did it on his school jumper! But we forgot to wash the bottle tops so it went all soggy and smelt and his mum went absolutely loopy! She was not at all happy! The pub was brick built and it was sideways onto the road. You went down a step and into the bar and there was a hatch for off-sales.

We used to help the milkman - William's Dairy. Job's Dairy was in School Road. Peter from William's Dairy would come round in an old brown milk float and if you helped him on a Saturday he would pay you half a crown which was a lot of money in those days *and* treat you to a bottle of Pepsi and a bag of crisps at the pub. He always used to stop at lunch time for his two pints. It was always a scramble to be first to help Peter. He came all the way down St Michael's Road and all the roads off it and at the end he'd give you half a crown from his leather pouch. It was wonderful! There was always a queue to join him on Saturday morning. He used to start at 8 o'clock, but we used to get there earlier because he could only take one boy at a time. There was one man who lived next to Valentine Woods whose wife was foreign. She used to have yoghurt and nobody knew what yoghurt was in those days. The milkman used to say, "Oh, it's just sour milk!" Milk in those days came in bottles with cardboard tops.

I remember Valentine Woods being in St Michael's Road. Some of their land was bought by the Council. They had a very narrow entrance and the big log lorries went down there to the saw mill. They used to do charcoal burning at the top of Sulham Hill. I remember back in the mid 60's when my father died and my mother had to go back to work she worked there for a while packing charcoal which they would send all over the world. Valentine Woods initially used to do big logs. It was run by a Polish chap and then they moved out to Aldermaston. We would buy off-cuts for the open fire. We didn't have central heating in those days.

Our school trip at Park Lane school was a picnic up Streatley Hill. We all met at Tilehurst railway station and Miss Wheeler took us all *en masse* up to Streatley Hill where we played games. As kids we used to cycle down Sulham Hill. There used to be a pair of old wooden stocks at the bottom of the hill where the telephone box is now. A bit further on is the stream and in the field is an old pillbox where we used to take sandwiches and just muck about in the stream. Sometimes we would cycle to Prospect Park to play football. In those days the surface of St Michael's Road was rough and where my mother lived there was a ditch in front of the house. In about 1955 they widened and re-surfaced the road. I was quite friendly with the steamroller driver, who lived in a corrugated tin 'shepherd's hut'. When I came home from Park Lane School he would be waiting at the end of St Michael's Road with the roller and he would let me drive the roller back, because his caravan was parked near my mother's house. It really impressed my mates! He was an Irishman, we used to call him Paddy. I would go along and talk to him in the evenings. He was a very educated chap. He had a book on handwriting and wherever he used to go he'd get people to write in his book. A couple of years later he was in the area again and he called in to see Mum. He was a really nice chap.

We used to play a lot in Blundells Copse. We called it the Moors. We'd take our bikes over there and do what we called 'tracking'. We didn't have BMX bikes in those days, but you could buy 'cow horn' handlebars and even knobbly tyres if you had a lot of money. We'd take the chain guard and the mudguards off and you had a tracking bike!

We used to go swimming at Arthur Hill's when we swam indoors. Sometimes we went to King's Meadow, but most of the time we went to the lido. But then there was the polio panic.

The Rex Cinema was our other favourite on a Saturday morning. It was a penny bus ride down to the Rex and 6d to get in and then you'd spend 1d on sweets and walk back. We used to tie our macs round our necks and think we were Superman. I remember as we reached the big concrete retaining wall opposite the Tyler's Rest pub up Norcot Hill where the buckets came across, if Superman had been the main film on Saturday morning we would walk up the wall to see who would walk up the farthest and jump off from the highest. My mate did it once and sprained his ankle. At the end of the film they would play the National Anthem and no-one wanted to stay to listen. The usherettes would stand at the end of the aisle stopping people from leaving. Everyone was trying to push past them. If it was your birthday you could go up on stage on Saturday morning and they would give you a ticket so you could get in free the following week. Nobody ever that I can remember got up there more than once a year.

I remember going to the Rex Cinema once with my two girl cousins who had come down from Kent and we saw *Carousel*. They were about 13 and 14 at the time and we watched this film twice through. They were in floods of tears all the way through and to this day it has put me off musicals. I can't stand them! I came out thinking what a rubbish film it was as there had been no cowboys in it and they thought it was wonderful. My grandmother was stood at the top of Grovelands Hill because we were late in her pinafores with her arms crossed!

Interviewed in June 1998

MRS GLADYS ABERY
(nee STACEY)
born 1908

formerly of Halls Road

I came to Tilehurst to live with my aunt, Mrs Harris (nee Stacey), who brought me up. We lived in a pair of thatched cottages in Halls Road, laid back off the road; at that time it was called Burnt Cottage but later it was changed to Rose Cottage. Great long path. We lived on the left-hand side and Mr and Mrs Kidd lived on the other side.

In the cottage we had paraffin lamps, a round table and the lamp in the middle; candles for upstairs. The bedroom doors were just a long plank of wood you know, with a hole to put your fingers through and lift up the latch.

Calcot Golf Club House used to be Lord and Lady Rosslyn's. When we were kids we used to go down there harvesting, making hay when you had the hay carts and the pitch forks and that sort of thing. They used to send sandwiches out and these great big jars of beer for the men and women, and lemonade for the children. I must have been about 11 years old. It was during the war because one of my aunts used to be in the Land Army, and she used to work on the land down there.

We used to go down Firs Road, down into the woods and all round the back of the fields and come out at the White Hart at Theale. You were knee deep in clay in the woods. Before you got to the White Hart you came to that other hill, Pincents. You'd come out halfway down there by the lime kiln. Lovegroves used to have that. You went round the corner and there was the White Hart.

There was another walk we used to do, out to the mill at Calcot. When we were kids we used to go, all the family, across the fields, across the railway, out by the Kennet and walk all along by the river and call in for a drink at the old Cunning Man. It was very interesting going across the fields and crossing the railway as many a time you had to listen out for the train coming along in case you got halfway across.

Broad Pool Pond used to be right opposite Park Farm and there was a great big pond where we'd go and get out tadpoles and frogs. They used to say that at certain times of the year it was haunted and you could see this ghost across the pond. We were scared stiff when we were kids to go up there because all along there was nothing but ditches. It was very watery, thick clay and everything.

The Blagraves had a hunting lodge in Halls Road. They had deer in the park then. There was also the old house called The Halls which was supposed to be haunted. The history we heard when we was younger was that the butler pushed the housemaid down the stairs and there is supposed to be blood stains still on the stairs. When we were kids we used to run like mad going past the house. I always remember that.

I was fourteen when I left school and I went into service. I left school on the Friday in the holiday term and I went straight into service on the Wednesday. I started off with Headingtons, the brewery people at Wokingham.

I was a general housemaid when I started, and had to do everything as I was all by myself. The daughter used to help me, but I used to have to do all the vegetables and the scrubbing, polishing, waiting at table and all this sort of thing.

From there I went to Horsley Towers in Surrey. I was in service with the Hon Mrs Sopwith. I was with them for a long time. There was twelve of us there; there was the stud groom, the gardeners, housemaids, parlourmaids, butler, housekeeper and the head butler. All the silver and all the cutlery and everything was in cupboards with green baize and big doors, and after every meal we had to wash the silver in hot soapy water then put them in another big sink with hot water, put them on the draining board, dry them and polish all of them before they went back.

We used to use soda in the washing up water, and we'd have to take the copper jugs up with the hot water to put in their hand basins so that they could wash. We maids used to have to go right up into the attic to our bedrooms. We had to be up no later than half past five, and down on our knees scrubbing floors and cleaning grates before breakfast. They were steel grates, and we used to have those burnishing gloves with the steel face. We had to steel all that and then about ten minutes later light the fire. You wouldn't think we had touched it about an hour afterwards.

At Horsley Towers when we were there, in the great assembly hall where they used to have banquets and everything, that was all stone floors. It used to take us girls three in a row to scrub this floor. The fireplace was a great huge thing laid back in all brickwork. They had these great big iron dogs and they used to burn a whole log going night and day. The brass heads of the dogs we had to clean whether they were hot or not. We used to have to polish those and if you left a little bit of Brasso in one of the eyes or any of the grooves, the housekeeper would come along and you had to do it all over again.

The housekeeper there was a real tartar. We'd have to spring clean everything, even the carpets had to come up and the gardeners had to take them down the garden and beat them. This particular day we were doing this room and we found a ring under the carpet. When we took it to the housekeeper she said she had put it there to see 'whether you girls were doing your job properly'.

At breakfast table we'd have whatever was going - the butler and housekeeper always had a whole kipper, but us maids had half a kipper each and you daren't ask for more, and the same for the evening meals. All the meals were served up, the butler used to carve the meat and then the housekeeper used to serve the vegetables.

We had a whole day off once a month, that was after you had done your work. You probably finished at eleven and had to be back by eight. I never got home much then. On the half day sometimes you would get away at three o'clock and you would have to be in at seven. At Horsley Towers we were very, very hard driven.

When I left Horsley Towers my aunt was supposed to meet me at the station. I passed her and she passed me. She didn't recognise me where I had got so thin. She kept me at home a month to get me built up, that was when I went to Ascot to Lord and Lady Linlithgow's. That wasn't their proper residence, the residence belonged to Lord and Lady Hope, but they used to let Lord and Lady Linlithgow have it for the racing season at Ascot. They used to sort of swap residences.

They'd go away to France for three months at a stretch. That was to their residence in France and while they were away we had to spring clean the house from top to bottom. Sometimes she would take some of her staff with her over there, the staff from France would come over to us. Take it in turns. Well I always remember when it was my turn to go, I came home and told my aunt and uncle, and my uncle said, "You're not going over there! It's not a fit place!" So I never went and had to stop at home with the other maids.

They were very good to us at Ascot. The half days that was from two o'clock and you had to be back in at nine o'clock, but you had to report to the Housekeeper. I used to bike from Ascot up to Tilehurst and back again in the evening. If the weather was bad I used to come by train. They were very good, whatever went in the dining room us servants had in the hall. When I left Ascot I was third housemaid there.

The poorest pay was at Headingtons. When I started at Wokingham I used to get 10/- a month, but at the Sopwiths at Horsley Towers I think it was about 12/-. When I left Ascot I was getting, I think, about £3 per month.,

When I left to get married I went to work for Mr and Mrs Harris who used to live in the lodge at the corner of Prospect Park and Honey End Lane. They used to breed Sealyham dogs.

My husband worked for Menpes, the fruit farm. When he was a boy and left school he went over there, and then as he got older the nursery closed down and he went to Kennet Valley Nurseries along the Burghfield Road, that used to belong to Sir Felix Pole. Then from there he came up and worked for Mr Peters along Halls Road, and then when Mr Peters died he finished his days out at Aldermaston as a messenger. The men were more or less all in the greenhouses or kilns - there wasn't much else for people to do.

At one time he had a job on the water tower. He was out of work for a long time when the nursery closed and then he went over there and helped to build that and Blagrave Hospital. I was an auxiliary at the hospital for eleven and a half years. Where all the houses are now, we used to sit on the bank there and watch the buildings going up. Frazers lived in the big house on the top of the hill. There was no houses in the woods. I know this because we used to follow the hounds all through the woods when we were kids.

When we were first married we went into a thatched cottage down by the church with a well outside the front door. It had a hook with buckets. We used to get all our water from the well in the middle of the path. Then we moved to another old thatched cottage in St Michael's Road by the Little Plough. My hubby's sister used to keep the little Plough. Our cottage had two rooms, one in and one up. The bedroom was like a landing and when my daughter was tiny we had a boarding put up and that made it into a room for her. The doors upstairs had a loop to put your fingers in, but the one downstairs had an ordinary latch. The cottage was very old. There was no back door. The thatch went down to about a foot off the back. The toilets used to be a bucket in the coal house in the shed. Then when you came in the front door you went into another little room which they called the pantry. It had a sink about 4" deep with a tap.

We never had a bathroom in any of the cottages and then when we moved to this house, well, it was just like a kid with a new toy. We had a bath nearly every night. We had had a tin bath at the cottage in St Michael's Road, and when we went into the little one down by the church we had one of those hip baths. We used to boil up the copper. The trouble was the copper was in the outshed. We'd fill it up with buckets, boil it up, bring it in in the buckets and then empty it again. Then with the toilet we used to have to come out of the front door, as there was no back door in either cottage, and go all the way round to the outshed to the toilet. They were buckets with wooden seats.

A lot of people calls me 'Abrey' and it's Abery. There's a lot of Aberys in Tilehurst.

Interviewed in May 1994 and January 1995

Cottage with well

MR LES RIXON
born 1927

formerly of Turnham's Farm

I was one of a large family. My father was an estate carpenter, he worked on various farms and in the early thirties moved to Turnham's Farm in City Road, Tilehurst. I would have been five or six at the time. We lived at the top of Pincent's Hill. In those days it was two cottages. These cottages enjoyed panoramic views over the Kennet Valley. Then of course there was no Savacentre or M4.

These cottages were subsequently bought by Bishop Whitehead as a retirement home. They were extensively refurbished and the residence is still there today. From Pincent's Hill my family moved to a brand new cottage, one of four in City Road not many yards from the actual farm. These cottages had running water and electric light, such modern conveniences were not the norm for many farm cottages in the early thirties. As young kids, almost as soon as we could walk we used to go out and collect wood to burn on the range. We did buy a certain amount of coal, but not very much. When I was a boy, in the farm cottage, the toilet was up the garden, which was usual. To go anywhere it was about a two mile walk to get to any form of public transport.

My father had a workshop on the farm and with very limited assistance and machinery built things like hay wagons which were used on the farm. Although my father had no formal training as a carpenter he was extremely adaptable and very clever with his hands.

When I was a little boy there was a family who used to play in a little three piece band at the village hall in Victoria Road. The chap used to get me to help him carry the bass drum, well he only had one leg. Some years later his widow rang me up and asked, "Do you know the sequel to that?" I said I didn't and she told me that they used to live in Recreation Road and the chap who moved in next to them also only had one leg and it was the other leg. Well this drummer used to work in Milwards in their little factory in Letcombe Street and periodically he would buy a pair of shoes and as they had the same size feet, he had the right one and this other bloke had the left one!

City Road had two shops. There was a little shop opposite the pub called Turner's. There was another one, it didn't last very long. That was a sweet shop. Then there was a vehicle repair business up there called Milton's.

The City was a little bit self-supporting even in those days. Parts of it were quite old and it was like going into another little different bit of Reading going out there. They had a football team, which my brother ran, called Tilehurst City. Every year they played Tilehurst which was the local big team in a charity match. It was very keenly fought over. Our team was sponsored by Bishop Whitehead whose wife was a very keen one to get the local community going in some form or other. She took this football team under her wing and of course like lads in a village they had an occasional swear after a game, but she frowned on that like a ton of bricks.

There was a bungalow, well a holiday home I suppose you should call it, in Normanstead Road and whoever owned it had some sort of affinity with the Boy Scouts. We couldn't believe our luck when he let us have use of that bungalow during the war as a sort of camping site and headquarters. There was a paddock and we camped in the woods next to it. Lionel Smee had it later

There were two quarries in Tilehurst. The one in Dark Lane was Maybough Pit. We used to play in that pit. The other one was by Pierce's Hill - they were both dug for chalk. There was also a sand pit in Pincent's Lane, part way down. It petered out at the end of the war, but it was quite good sand. They were little bits of local industry.

In conjunction with the blockhouse that they built during the war they built a huge trench, an anti-tank ditch. It must have been at least eight foot deep. It ran from not quite Pangbourne almost up to where Savacentre is. It ran roughly above Nunhide Lane, but it was huge. As kids we wondered what on earth they were doing. It was regarded as a second or third line of defence. They built blockhouses all over the place. There was one at the top of Sulham Hill, that one has gone now, but the ones down by Nunhide are still there. It was a huge anti-tank trench, through the fields. It was dug at the greatest possible speed because they were expecting an invasion.

Interviewed in December 1996

Turnham's Farm circa 1974

Highland Cattle in Westwood Glen!

MRS DOROTHY BROCKS
born 1918

formerly of Chapel Hill

I lived down Chapel Hill (from Littleheath direction), just before you get to Lower Elmstone Drive. There's an unmade lane which goes down to the Royal Oak pub and I lived in one of the three cottages which are still there. Holly Cottage is at the back and was originally a pair of cottages. Mrs Strong lived in one and two elderly brothers lived in the other one, then when Wickens bought the farm he made them into one for his sons to live in. Then there was Laurel Cottage which was my husband's old home where he was born in 1901. His elder brother, Frank, lived there until some years ago when he died, aged 92. My husband's father owned the three cottages; the two that got made into one and Laurel Cottage, the old home. He gave no. 58 to my husband as a wedding present and he sold the rest. There was another one further down the hill which they pulled down - Mr and Mrs Burgess lived there. It was demolished when they put in Lower Elmstone Drive. I would think the cottages must be about 130 years old now. There is a date on them in the bricks between my old cottage and the next one, but you may not be able to see it now with the Snowcem all over it. They were tied cottages originally. It was farm land and the workers lived in them. It was Firpit Farm which was worked properly as a farm before the Wickens took it over. I don't know who owned it before the Wickens family. The Wickens were a very old Tilehurst family.

We drew all our water from a well. We had a chemical toilet, no mains drainage. All six cottages shared the well which was on Mr

Wickens' ground until the water was declared to be unfit for human consumption and we had to go on the mains. We never had a flush toilet until the 1950's. We had gas when we first moved into the cottage; electricity didn't come until the late 1940's. I had a washhouse separate from the cottage.

The land in front of the cottage was Tilehurst Poor Land and there are still two allotments there. Then the Tilehurst Poor sold off the other land and built the houses on the other side of the lane (Felton Way). They took part of the allotment land to make the path up Chapel Hill.

We lived in Chapel Hill from 1937 until 1982. There was a Baker family in Chapel Hill. One of their daughters married Jack Brereton of the grocery family. Mrs Adlam used to live on the top of the hill before you started to go down. Her cottage protruded out onto the hill and had to be demolished and two houses were put up in the grounds afterwards. Mr Adlam, an old Reading man had been a policeman in Brighton and when he retired he and his wife wanted to come back this way. They had waited so long to get the cottage that they called it, 'At Last'.

The Chapel was never used as such in my time - it was a house. It was more or less opposite the lane where our cottage was. The Powells lived there, they were stonemasons. He used to make headstones. His business was on the other side of town, in the Wokingham Road.

When I moved to Tilehurst in 1937 and you turned in the lane where I lived there was nothing over Chapel Hill, it was all fields and there were just two bungalows up Normanstead Road, which was an unmade road. Francis Bros had just finished building those detached houses which end at Normanstead Road.

There were a couple of cottages in Westwood Glen and my sister-in-law lived in one. It backed onto the field with a stream where they used to have the Highland Cattle. My sister-in-law and her husband owned the fields round there. They used to rent out one of the fields to Stevens the butcher for his daughter to keep her pony in.

Interviewed in March 1995

MR REGINALD BUTLER
born 1921

formerly of Chapel Hill

It was in 1927 when my family moved from Reading to Chapel Hill, Tilehurst. In those days you had the old pantechnicon with the horses to move you, wooden pantechnicons with hard wheels. I remember we had to stop half way up Norcot Hill. That was when it was three deliberate hills and we had to stop to change horses.

Francis the builders in Tilehurst had just started building six detached houses on the second hill. My parents bought the first house which was the show house for the princely sum of £550 - a fortune in those days. My father worked at Huntley and Palmers for 48/- a week, so it must have been very hard for them in those days, but they made it. There were five of us, my mother, father, grandmother, my sister Nora and myself. Those houses are still there today. In those days Chapel Hill, like so many other roads, was just a gravel track.

At the top of Chapel Hill there were the following families: the Kirtons (Dolly), Strongs, Chapmans, Roses, Richardsons, Granny Smith to mention a few. On the brow of the hill were Mr and Mrs Adlam, a retired policeman and on the opposite side were the Hazell family and the Thimblebys. At the bottom of the hill was the Smith family, travelling people, Romanies, a wonderful, kind family. They lived in a bungalow with a lot of land with two lovely genuine romany caravans used by the family. After the war, Mr Smith organised a street party for all in the fields opposite, which is now all houses and a road. At the bottom of the hill there was a stream which went under the road. Goodness knows what happened to that because there is a mini roundabout there now which gives Chapel Hill a dog leg where it was always a straight road. Going up the other part of the hill there was only hedges, allotments and fields, until you reached the top on the left where there was the chapel from which, of course, it got its name. Next was a large field and then my parents' home and my home for many, many years.

I remember the line of oak trees in Park Lane at the top of Chapel Hill. How many times did we climb the trees from school and tear our trousers? Little shorts we had on in those days. Up Park Lane on the left-hand side was Edgar Newbery (not Arthur Newbery) who had a big farm there, then of course you went off down City Road, a gravel road, not made up. The circus came there once a year, and every year we used to have a fire because there was a lot of gorse on Park Farm. That was in the days when we had the seasons and you knew you were going to get some sun. The old fire engines would be out and we'd love it, of course. It was only fields before they built the houses up there and it was the *old* water tower in those days. There was a big pond known as Whirlpool. It was said that it sucked in animals.

I went to Park Lane School and later to Norcot School, passing through Miss Drew's class (she loved to rap your knuckles with the ruler) Mr Turner's and, of course, Mr Saul's class (a deadly shot with odd pieces of chalk.) Mr Eyles was the headmaster in my day. Mr Saul being the sports master made History and Geography lessons very interesting coupling them with football, cricket, in fact any sport. I played football for Norcot Senior and Reading Boys and in 1935 my last year at school we won the 5-a-side winners' gold medal at Aston Tirrold. We were very proud of that achievement particularly as no master had accompanied us.

In School Road there was Bishop's the chemist and at Christmas he displayed toys in the window. In either 1929 or 1930 I saw a toy car, which you wound up in the front, put it in gear and it would go forwards or backwards. In those days one could only look and dream of such pleasures because of the expense. Imagine my surprise when on Christmas Day I opened my present and there it was - and I still have it today, that special toy I saw in Bishop's window.

Also in School Road was Barefoot's cycle shop. What a grand man Mr Barefoot was. If we school children had a problem with our cycles, it was never too much trouble for him to put things right and many a time he forgot to say how much it was. Often people would come to collect their bikes after repair and say they didn't have the money and that they'd just go home and get it and he'd say, "Oh forget it, don't bother!"

There were the Champions, Bubbles and her brother. Bubbles became a masseuse. There was Old Ma Champion and Mr Champion who worked at Simonds Brewery. He used to ride what we called a saddle tank motorbike in those days and when he got on it you couldn't see the bike because he was a huge person. Her place was round behind the church and there was a huge great tree in the front. She always had jars of sweets. You'd go round and say, "Can I have a ha'porth or farthing's worth and she'd come out and load a bag up with sweets. Smashing people.

In my school days I did a paper round for Winchcomb's, the shop on the corner of Westwood Road and Park Lane, the crossroads by the Triangle, that was. My Sunday round was a marathon. I started delivering in Norcot Road, then Norcot Hill, Church End Lane, Halls Road, Firs Road through to the City, Little Heath, Chapel Hill and back to the shop. In those days we used to collect the money each week as well. Cold job in the winter, but Tilehurst was a healthy place.

In the old days in the City you had the almshouses, two farms and the good old Fox and Hounds pub and a garage opposite.

How many remember the old National School building in School Road? I joined the Cubs there. And the Police Box outside where our local bobbies, PC Skinner and PC Groves, had their cup of tea and sandwich and called the main Police Station in Reading - in those days it was in Valpy Street.

The policemen in Tilehurst in those days were good coppers. If they caught you doing anything wrong, they'd clip you round the ear'ole and you took notice of them. We had the old gas lamps then and it was wonderful to throw a stone and break the glass in the lamp and then of course the mantle got blown out too. We weren't goody-goodies, but if they caught you doing it you were frightened to death. They'd say that next time they'd tell your parents and that was terrible.

I used to get caught on the building sites. I loved going on building sites; we would climb ladders. They didn't have cement then. They had lime pits in those days. They had the sand, the lime pit and they mixed all their own mortar. They put hair with it. That was in the good old days of lathe and plaster walls. They used to put the laths across when they made a ceiling or walls.

I went to the Methodist Church in School Road and after I left the cubs my father, together with Reverend Rutter, formed the 4th Tilehurst Boys' Brigade. Rev Rutter was the preacher at the Methodist Chapel in School Road and we held all our meetings in the hall behind the Chapel. My mother made the banner for the Brigade with the BB badge and motto and it was kept in the Chapel unless we were out marching. She used to do a lot of embroidery and tapestry. We had some wonderful times there. Their sermons were not 'heavy' and their hymns were great. The Lascelles went there and the Herberts. A lot of people went there. We had great fun in the holidays. What was then the highlight for us - you'd catch the charabanc in those days and we'd go to Bucklebury Common or Goring and Streatley, up Streatley Hill and to Bradfield Common. It was terrific. I had wonderful times with the Methodist Church. After I left I think the Tilehurst Boys' Brigade amalgamated with a Boys' Brigade company from Reading. I was a Sunday School teacher at the end of my time there. In those days we *had* to go to Sunday School but it wasn't a chore, you enjoyed it.

Unfortunately Reverend Rutter was quite a young man when he died. That was sad because everybody loved him. He was a nice person. Then we had Pastor Burns. He loved to tell us his life story. He had been a down-and-out, on the roads. He got this calling and he joined and passed all his exams and he was a terrific guy, full of fun and joined in everything, a great character. I can't remember who came after him.

Edgar Newbery was a member of the Methodist Church. Arthur Newbery who owned the gorgeous furniture store in Reading owned Daneshill which was off the Oxford Road down by the Roebuck. When he died Mr Smith, who owned Smith's coaches, bought Daneshill. They'd open Daneshill every spring - they had lovely do's there. Smithy carried it on after he bought it from Arthur Newbery.

Edgar Newbery used to run outings for the younger people in the Methodist Chapel. There were trips up the river, little seminars and you'd hop off at Mapledurham.

We used to go to TocH just opposite St Michael's Church. Service personnel could go there and get a cup of tea. You could stay there if you were on your way somewhere, they would put you up. They'd feed you, like the Salvation Army. The symbol of TocH was a little lamp, like Aladdin's lamp, with a small flame coming out of the spout. The brick hut outside the Church was put up during the war and it was a pillbox. It was tucked behind the wall and you could only look down the hill towards Cockney Hill. You couldn't look up the hill as the wall came out and blocked the view. It was used by the LDV before they became the Home Guard.

There are so many memories one can recall of those years I spent at Tilehurst: picking cowslips at Killhorse, the piggeries in Park Lane, the copse and woods, which is now Warborough Avenue and the estate. The original two old houses that were in the middle of the woods are still standing and occupied. My sister and her husband lived in one of them, many years ago.

Interviewed in March 1999

Picking cowslips at Killhorse

MR BILL STOKES
1911 - 1998

formerly of Oak Tree Road

My wife and I moved to 'Oaktree', Oaktree Road Tilehurst at the end of the war in the Autumn of 1945. At this time there was only a small hut on the other side of the road. It belonged to the lady who owned this house, a Mrs Milner, whose mother had lived here in 1900 and earlier. This house was a small farmhouse and there were two dwellings (known as the Cottages) which were later converted into a single house. Our house was originally very small, dating back to the eighteenth century. Mrs Milner had the back of the house extended as can be clearly seen today.

The stables and water well are still in use, but the old barn collapsed and has been rebuilt as a garage. There were no other houses near and the land opposite was an open space adjoining Arthur Newbery Park. The house (which was converted from the two cottages) was occupied by a Mr Brain and when he left it was taken over by Dr Mitchell whose father was the designer of the Spitfire. Dr Mitchell's property has now become 'Oaktree Copse' with an exit onto Overdown Road. In all seven large houses have been built on the site.

What really changed the face of Tilehurst was when Overdown Road came through the valley from the 'Roundabout' public house on the Oxford Road right up to the area near the water tower.

interviewed in November 1996

Crashed German bomber

MR ERIC BORHAM
born 1929

Westwood Road

I came as an evacuee to Reading in 1945 when war broke out and stayed with a Mrs Franklin in Albany Road off the Oxford Road. After two years her husband was called up and she started work so in 1941 when I was twelve I came to live at a boys' hostel opposite Tilehurst Station. It was run by a Matron and a Sister and there were about a dozen of us boys. It was one of those big houses with its own tennis court and a garage half sunk in the ground. They kept about a hundred chickens. They treated us well.

While I was still at Albany Road they shot a German bomber down which landed in Prospect Park. We got there before the Home Guard. I had perspex out of that aircraft. We kids heard it crash and were all up there like a shot. The pilot had bailed out. It was a two-seater bomber with double propellers.

Interviewed in March 1993

Auntie Rose cleaning the war memorial

MRS DORIS CARTER
(nee HODGE)
born 1928

Westwood Road

I came to Tilehurst on 1 September 1939, two days before war broke out. I stopped with my aunt and uncle, Rose and Jim Lovegrove at 21 School Road. We stopped down here until just before Christmas 1939 and, as there was no trouble as regards bombing in London, we went back. It was in October 1940 that we were bombed out, so we came back to Tilehurst.

As evacuees - we were private - but most of the others came from West Hill School, Putney and from North Holmes School in Canterbury. A lot of them were billeted with people in Lyndhurst Road and Thirlmere Avenue because the estates were all down there. But they all had to come up to Norcot School from 9.00 am - 11.00 am every day then to the Congregational Church in Armour Road from 11.30 am - 12.30pm for more lessons. Then we went to the National School each Friday for assembly, then to Park Lane School for our music lessons. We dug for victory in Wardle Avenue because there were allotments down Wardle Avenue where the bowling green is now. This was part of our schooling, to help the war effort. In the summer we went up to Hall Place Farm to stook corn and give a hand in general. We had fun.

We had trips to the old Rex Cinema at the bottom of Norcot Hill (the best seat in the house was 1/6d!) that was a highlight. But we had to go to the pictures early as the last bus up Norcot Hill was at 9.00pm or walk all the way home up Norcot Hill past Minchin's Farm which was by Lawrence's Estate, and very dark in the blackout. Minchin's Farm was where Broomfield Road is now.

We never had any fear of walking up Norcot Road even in the 1940's when the whole distance of the road to the Meadway was bordered by Ranikhet Camp. There were 3,000 American servicemen in it - 327th Glider Infantry attached to the 101st American Airborne Division. A lot of them came up to the Methodist Church because it had a Youth Club and facilities for games there. During the time they were here, quite a lot of Tilehurst girls became GI brides. There was never any trouble. Unfortunately we were a bit too young and my Dad forbade me to go out with any of them! A lot of them were killed on D- Day. Then Christmas 1944, they were at the Battle of Bastogne and held out against the Germans for a week. A lot of them were at Nijmegen.

Auntie Rose used to keep the old War Memorial clean - she'd go to the National School with her scrubbing brush and bucket and scouring powder. Mrs Marsh would give her a bucket of hot water to clean it with. The Memorial used to be in the middle of the road.

During the war, every other Wednesday, we paid 6d to dance to a wind-up gramophone in the Village Hall. On a Saturday night they had a resident live band there.

Interviewed in March 1993

MRS JUNE LUSH
(nee MANNING)
born 1931

formerly of Calcot

I was born in St Michael's Road at my Grannie's but I spent my childhood in Calcot. I have only memories of Verandah Cottages. Mrs Boseley the washer woman lived next door. She was a lovely old lady, I called her Bo. She used to do my mother's washing. I loved staying with her. She would push an old pram about with the washing in, collecting and delivering the fresh laundered washing. Bo had a copper in an outbuilding where she did her washing. She had an outside toilet and no bathroom, and we shared an outside tap between the two cottages.

My friend and I used to attend Sunday School at the Mission Hall. Mr Reed the village policeman had the house next door to it. The Mission Hall has now been converted into a very attractive house.

Calcot Post Office was run by Mr and Mrs Tommie Wise. He was a little old man. Mrs Wise was very tall and very prim and proper.

My father was born in 1894 and his parents ran the Traveller's Friend at the bottom of Langley Hill. My own parents took the pub over in about 1922. I don't know how long they ran it but my mother hated it. They eventually moved to a house called Crossway where I spent my childhood. I remember lots of open fields where my father and grandfather kept cattle. We always had picnics in the hayfield, and lots of lovely walks, especially on Sunday afternoons when Dad took me to look at his cattle in Reeve's orchard which was opposite Calcot Post Office. We also went on walks down the path to Calcot Mill.

When my grandfather died in 1953, my parents moved to Firlands, the farm at the top of Langley Hill. I didn't live there as I got married in that same year. My father kept mainly pigs and some cattle. He employed a man called Bunker who actually looked after the farm. In the war bombs fell on my grandfather's dairy and several came down in the fields down Langley Hill.

Originally Firlands was the hunting lodge for Calcot Park (now Calcot Golf Club) belonging to the Blagrave family. In Firlands there was a beautiful panelled gun room with cupboards where the guns were kept. Unfortunately it has now been pulled down along with Blagrave Hospital.

Interviewed in November 1994

Washday

MR LES HAWKINS
1908 - 1999

Calcot Row

I went to school at Grovelands. When the 1914-18 war broke out Battle Hospital was still the workhouse, but after the battle of the Somme they turned it into a war hospital and the workhouse moved to Grovelands School. So then we had to go to school at Tilehurst. We went to Norcot School half day. On our way to school we would go along the side of the golf course, a nine hole golf course, and if there was any golf balls come our way we used to tread them in and we would have them coming home! You couldn't pick them up or the golfers would be after you. We used to tread them in and hope they would still be there. After the war when I was nearly leaving school we came back to Grovelands for a little while.

I started work at fourteen with Colliers. I did all manner of jobs and I finished up as brick moulder, you know, the hand-made moulding, the posh bricks for the posh houses. The Shakespeare Memorial Theatre was built of our bricks. They were hand-made and they were specially burnt a browny colour. They used to fire the kilns with tar and all manner of things. It filled the buildings, choked you nearly, a terrible job it was. I was called up two years later than I should have been as we had a special contract to make bricks for the air raid shelters in Reading.

I got married in 1929 and my father-in-law was Mr Hunt that used to have the builders opposite the Horn & Castle. He had a workshop there, a carpenters and a wheelwright. My mother-in-law had the little grocers shop as you go up New Lane Hill. My father-in-law was chauffeur to Lady Blagrave at Calcot Park in his early days when the first cars were invented. They bought a Mercedes Benz I think. That was the poshest car at that time so they say and my father-in-law learnt to drive it. The Lady wouldn't let her husband drive it. He had to do the job. When the Blagraves moved away they gave him the contract to keep all the Blagrave houses in repair. At that time they owned about half the houses in Reading.

Thackery had a farm down Mill Lane in Calcot and ran coaches from Newbury to London and you could pick them up to Reading from the Bath Road. He sold it to Thames Valley and they ran a better service.

Tilehurst had the reputation of being a rough place; you went up there for a dust up and the City was worse than that! The Fox and Hounds had a bit of a reputation.

interviewed in February 1994

The Fox and Hounds, City Road

MEMORIES OF PARK LANE SCHOOL

by George Critchell

Living almost opposite at the Prince of Wales public house, I was enrolled at Park Lane School on 27th March 1916. Instruction was very formal, the cane was used fairly liberally. A lasting impression was made on my mind at an early age and I made a mental note not to incur the Head's wrath.

There was no main entrance as there is today, and the present school hall which fronts Downing Road and the flat roofed extension towards Chapel Hill did not then exist. Gates from School Road gave access to the two playgrounds, and between these gates there was an enclosed plantation along the front of the school known as "the shrubbery" which pupils were forbidden to enter. There were lime trees on the edge of the playgrounds along the School Road and Downing Road frontages, and in the late Summer it was unwise to stand under these trees because of the danger of being stung by falling wasps, sated by the limes. A tarmac path led from each gate to the back of the building, and entry to the school was through lobbies containing coat pegs and wash basins into a long corridor. At each end of the corridor there was a long room divided into two teaching areas by a tall curtain, and there were three other classrooms along the front of the building. In all the teaching areas except those occupied by the infants, the floors were tiered and pupils sat in pairs in metal framed wooden desks including bench seats.

The infant classes were at the Downing Road end so promotion from the Infants to Standard I meant a change to the opposite end of the building, where desks were tiered. The school bell, which in those days was rung for several minutes continuously before the start of each school day, was operated by a rope and as soon as the bell stopped ringing pupils lined up in the playground and marched in for morning assembly. For the older pupils this took place to musical accompaniment, played by one of the pupils on the piano. When Florence Mandrell left the school I took over this daunting task.

There were two separate gravel surfaced playgrounds divided by a high brick wall and astride the wall was an open shelter under which we assembled before being marched into school. The open air sanitary offices were situated on the edge of the playgrounds furthest from the school and, there being no main drainage, the receptacles under the seats consisted of either a trough or large buckets. The playground on the Downing Road side was for girls and infants and the other was for boys. In the latter there was a high horizontal metal bar some six feet high between two wooden posts. In my time I witnessed some astonishing feats known as the 'Muscle Grimes'. A boy would hang from it by the crook of his elbows, with hands in pockets, and swing backwards and forwards until he had generated sufficient momentum to somersault. Understandably two or three somersaults were as much as a boy could manage in one performance. The few who did were tough characters.

We enjoyed little by way of organised sport and we compared unfavourably with Norcot School where enthusiasts such as 'Solly' Saul and 'Quacker' Drake were on the staff.

In those days Park Lane School had an extensive catchment area. A substantial number of pupils lived in the immediate vicinity of the school, but from further afield all the children from the City, then an isolated community around the Fox and Hounds public house, came to Park Lane because it was the nearest school. Alf Ilsley, the carrier in School Road, used to convey pupils form Calcot and back because the little school at Calcot had been closed. Others came to Park Lane by parental choice from the Armour Road and Kentwood Hill areas, although Norcot School may have been nearer.

It is sad to record that with the exception of Theale, all the other schools in the Tilehurst School Board's original district have disappeared, with Norcot too, but there is so far no threat to the future of Tilehurst Park Lane County Primary School. *Floreat semper*!

Park Lane School outing to Streatley Hill circa 1935/6 including Rosemary Remnant, Bernard Starkes, Dennis Gill, Norman Bowyer, Leslie Howard, ? Cooper, Mike Jessup, Daphne ?, Gwen Duffin, Margaret Turner, Valerie Hall

Norcot School Teachers circa 1920
Back row: Mr Saul, Miss Upstone, Mr Saxby (Headmaster),
Miss Cox, Mr Drake
Front row: Miss Ferris, ?, Miss Goodger, Miss Holloway

NORCOT SCHOOL TEACHERS

"Mr Saul was a strict old thing and I was so glad I wasn't a boy. He would take them by the ear and throw them about. He yelled his head off; you could hear him all over Tilehurst - he was mad on football and music." **Mrs Olive Lascelles.**

"If you were sent to Mr Saxby for being in trouble you had the cane across your hand then he would give you a comic to read! I always remember that Mr Eyles took over, Frank Eyles. He came in about 1925. Up to then we didn't do any writing, we was all printing with a pencil. Then he made us do writing. I stayed at Norcot from five to fourteen. There was Mr Saul, he was very strict. If you was talking in class he would chuck a pencil box at you, a lump of chalk was nothing. You wouldn't do it now, he was a very strict bloke. He loved his sport. He used to have a good football team in them days. I left in 1930 and he was just a teacher then *(He became headmaster in 1940.)* Mr Saul was there a very long time because when he left they gave him a television set. All the kids were collecting. That was a marvellous thing in them days. He lived in Norcot Road opposite the school. He was over ninety when he died."
   Ken Englefield

"When we came out of school, right opposite the school into Norcot School there was an entrance going to the kilns, the pits, and we used to walk down there back into Saul's house (he was the headmaster) and we had to dig his garden. He had a beautiful garden and a beautiful house up there. I have never known anyone to have such neat handwriting as him. On the blackboard he would do it quick, but you couldn't fault it. I can picture him now, he looked a bit like Will Hay! He was clever and very strict! He didn't wear a gown, just a suit and always immaculately dressed. Then we had another one called Mr Drake, he was an older chap, but in them days you respected the teacher, 'Yes Sir!' and 'No Sir!'."
   Roy Stamp